A **UDL** *NOW!* book

Universal Design for Learning in English Language Arts

Improving Literacy Instruction Through Inclusive Practices

KATIE NOVAK, RYAN HINKLE, BRIANNE PARKER, JINA POIRIER, AND ANNE WOLFF

© 2024 CAST, Inc.

ISBN (paperback): 978-1-943085-08-8
ISBN (ebook): 978-1-943085-09-5
Library of Congress Control Number: 2023944579

Cover design: Lindie Johnson
Interior design: Happenstance Type-O-Rama

"I Love the Look of Words" was first published in *Soul Looks Back in Wonder*, Tom Feelings, Ed. New York: Puffin. Copyright ©1993 by Maya Angelou.

Published by CAST Professional Publishing, an imprint of CAST, Inc., Lynnfield, Massachusetts, USA
For information about special discounts for bulk purchases, please email publishing@cast.org or visit publishing.cast.org.

To all the educators who believe in the power of literacy to open worlds and change lives, this is for you.

Contents

Introduction

The Power of Hypercolor, the A-Team, and UDL

Katie Novak

In middle school, I begged my parents for a Hypercolor shirt. If you aren't a child of the early '90s, you may not be aware of the fad, which fizzled out like a shooting star. The Hypercolor T-shirt was only available from 1993 to 1995, and then, the manufacturer went bankrupt. It's not hard to figure out why.

In theory, Hypercolor was amazing. What appeared to be a hot pink T-shirt would magically change colors based on body heat. I imagined pressing my sweaty hands against the side of the shirt to make a blue peace sign, a high-five, or even my initials. Brilliant. Welp, until you realized that the sweat beneath your armpits would also change colors. Fad over. Or so I thought.

As I was researching the demise of Hypercolor T-shirts, I found that a company on Amazon has resurrected the heat-sensitive color-shifting shirt. I literally cringed when I saw photos of the Shadow Shifter, with their swirls of pink and purple, like wearable cotton candy. Turns out, the reviews are excellent! One reviewer, Vanessa, promised, "If you miss the '80s fashion trend you'll be happy to know the technology has improved and these shirts are great!" So, the moral of the story is, you live and you learn. I have experienced the same in my UDL practice.

When *UDL Now!* was written in 2014, it was meant to be a playbook for designing curriculum and instruction to meet the needs of the widest variety of learners. The focus was on all students, preK–12, and how teachers could co-design learning experiences that were flexible enough for each student to reach high expectations as they worked toward grade-level standards. As with the Hypercolor shirt, the proverbial stains started to surface and I realized that an overhaul was necessary. Goodness gracious, I have learned so much since I wrote the first edition, which speaks to the evolution of our profession and the power of lifelong learning.

UDL Now!, in its third edition, provides a much deeper look at Universal Design for Learning (UDL) and its connection to multitiered systems, equity, and inclusive practice. However, for many teachers, questions still nag, and often those questions are subject-specific. When working with English language arts teachers, I continually hear, "But what does UDL look like in an English language arts class? Does it allow for shared reading and novel studies? And if so, what does that look like?" And most often, "How do we get our students to engage in their literacy lives when we're competing with TikTok and chatbots?"

The answers to these questions are critical in scaling UDL. Research from the Institute for Education Sciences (IES, 2016) suggests that although intensive content-focused professional development (PD) improves teachers' content knowledge, it doesn't translate into improvements in student achievement. Therefore, content area PD needs to be delivered through the lens of a pedagogical framework like UDL. A report from the Learning Policy Institute (Darling-Hammond, Hyler, & Gardner, 2017) doubles down on the research and also notes that effective professional learning has an intentional focus on discipline-specific curriculum development as well as pedagogies. This book aims to fill this gap by explicitly connecting English language arts curriculum and pedagogies through the lens of UDL. In short, we aim to answer the aforementioned questions.

As a teacher of English, I implemented UDL in my classroom for years, which resulted in increased mastery and engagement. Before I implemented UDL, many of my students seemed disengaged. If I had a dollar for every time a teenager paired, "Why are we doing this?" with a groan and sigh, well, you know how that sentence ends! Many students rushed through their work as though there were a prize for the fastest and messiest finish, if they did the work at all. I was definitely trying too hard to get them interested and excited to learn, but the commitment wasn't always there. In short, they didn't seem to care very much about learning. However, after I began to implement UDL strategies, I noticed a significant improvement in their engagement and motivation to learn. They began to look forward to class and at times even groan when class was over, whining that they wanted to stay with me alllllllll day.

One particular example speaks to the power of deep and authentic learning. The assignment was to create a representation of Freytag's pyramid to help peers visualize how elements in a chosen story interacted to drive the plot. Together, we unpacked the standard, created success criteria, and designed a rubric. After that, the students did all the work. I told them they were welcome to share their learning in any way, as long as it incorporated all the success criteria. One student, Nick, used leather burning tools to create a stunning piece of artwork that exemplified the plot structure and literally inspired numerous classmates to try to replicate.

This level of creativity and mastery was not uncommon among my students after I began to implement UDL.

Providing multiple options for learning and assessment gave my students more control of their own learning, which in turn motivated them to take risks, put in effort, and collaborate and share themselves and their strengths with classmates. Not only did I observe a significant improvement in their mastery of standards, but the class was so much easier to manage, kids seemed to get along better, and overall, I didn't have to be the human fun-meter, trying to build shallow engagement with bad jokes!

That being said, the students in my classroom weren't particularly difficult to engage. Most were compliant, and most of their basic needs were being met. I have worked with countless educators who serve, and struggle with how to inspire, students facing more significant barriers, such as chronic stress and trauma, unstable living conditions, and less access to technology, books, or other materials that are essential for learning.

All this is challenging enough, and then the robots started coming for us. Solutions like ChatGPT and all its cousins have the potential to tempt students with easy solutions that prevent true engagement, critical thinking, and deep relationships with humans. So, all in all, being an English teacher today is a lot. Believe me, I get it.

Four years ago, while consulting, I met an amazing team of literacy educators at an alternative high school program. In the program, their colleagues refer to them as the "A-Team." These educators serve students in alternative schools, judicial schools, military schools, and makeshift hotel schools. Together, they've served learners who have faced the most significant challenges and barriers to learning, and worked with them to eliminate barriers through design. Too often, people think of UDL as requiring expensive technology and flashy classrooms that look like a Google office space. My co-authors, without access to those systemic drivers, have helped students to realize academic success, increased engagement, and growth in all literacy domains. They created spaces where their students had what they needed to learn at high levels by building authentic relationships with learners, promoting student voice and choice, and connecting English language arts instruction to the lived experiences of the students they serve. When we connected and they shared how they met, I knew I needed to collaborate with them.

How the A-Team Assembled

In the movie *Anchorman*, Will Ferrell's character, Ron Burgundy, grabs a conch shell and shouts, "News Team, assemble!" Our team may not have had a conch shell, but upon reflection, we realized we had a common denominator, Jina with a *J*.

Jina was out of the classroom and working as a program specialist in our English language learner (ELL) department. The program specialist position provided Jina with the unique opportunity to work alongside the teachers throughout our district. Our district, being geographically vast, is great for students, as they can access schools near their homes, but before Zoom and virtual meetings, these scattered sites didn't make it easy for staff members to collaborate. Brianne and Jina spent many years with only a door between their individual classrooms. Through years of teaching together and collaborating with both the English language arts (ELA) and ELL committees, Brianne and Jina were in the teacher-bestie zone! Come on, y'all know exactly what we mean when we talk about "teacher bestie" status. The person you can safely throw ideas out to and know it's okay to fail in front of. The person who has your back when it comes to sub plans. However, the most important feature of a teacher bestie is that they are the one place you can go to vent, gossip, and keep it real.

Next, Ryan entered the mix. How did Ryan end up as the only man on a team of strong females? If you ask Ryan, he will say it was penance for some poor choices in adolescence.

While Jina and Brianne were deep in BFF land, Ryan was displaced from his previous school. Due to decreased enrollments, Ryan was transferred to a new site and was assigned to share a room with none other than Mrs. Brianne Parker. Want a great story about first impressions? Ryan called Brianne the ice princess after he first met her. Jina's first memory was that Ryan had a penchant for puka shell necklaces (she thought they went out of style, but apparently Ryan brought them back!).

Now for the fourth and final member of the team. Brianne, Jina, and Ryan were a part of the ELA curriculum committee. As the educational technology expert, Anne supported the curriculum committee using her ed tech chops. Anne's first impression of Ryan was a bit harsher than Jina's puka shell diss. If we're being honest, her opinion was rooted in the fact that Ryan would turn in his lessons on a Word document and not a Google doc. Sidenote: Ryan is now a Google Certified Educator Level 1, but he still prefers to use WordPerfect.

We were one big happy work committee when our assistant superintendent posed a challenge to our crew: Find a new curriculum to support the inclusion of high-interest novels into ELA courses while incorporating UDL, social-emotional learning, character education, and restorative practices—or create one. Ryan searched endlessly on multiple educational websites and in textbooks but wasn't able to find anything that seemed current or enlightening. Every resource for novels was virtually the same: comprehension questions and vocabulary. It was clear: We had to design the curriculum program ourselves.

We've all heard the saying, "Everything happens for a reason." Some have described us as lightning in a bottle. Others have described us as mud in a flask, but that is the minority opinion (although we do love that simile!). While reminiscing about how we all met and became the "A-Team" of integrating UDL, social-emotional learning, character education, and restorative practices into our ELA curriculum, we all agreed that we consider ourselves lucky that our paths crossed and we were able to develop a team that works so harmoniously together. We feel so lucky to be able to share what we have learned with you. Consider us extended members of your PLC!

* * *

As soon as I met the A-Team and they shared their origin story, I was struck by how they applied the UDL framework to their ELA instruction while integrating other inclusive practices like social-emotional learning, restorative practices, and character education. I thought, *These are the people who I want to work with to scale the UDL message!*

We collaborated on this book to share how to universally design literacy instruction while also supporting the social, emotional, and behavioral health of students and helping them to embrace their identity and character in a restorative and engaging community. Connecting the dots by integrating all of these frameworks in our lesson delivery is how we can get as close to "doing it all" as possible.

ELA classrooms are particularly important for the application of these frameworks because literacy is a foundational skill that impacts every area of a student's life. In order to be successful in school and in the broader world, students must be able to read, write, speak, and listen effectively. However, traditional approaches to literacy instruction have often been one-size-fits-all models and haven't taken into account the diverse needs and backgrounds of students. Furthermore, ELA classrooms provide a unique opportunity to explore the human experience through literature, writing, and communication. Our content is ideal for integrating social-emotional learning and character education, which focus on developing empathy, self-awareness, and positive character traits. By using texts that address social-emotional themes and ethical dilemmas, we help students make connections between their own experiences and those of others. Writing prompts and authentic assessments that encourage self-reflection and self-expression can help students develop a deeper understanding of their own emotions and perspectives, while collaborative learning activities can promote positive communication, collaboration, and community.

ELA classrooms are also well suited for restorative practices. Literature that addresses conflict resolution, forgiveness, and reconciliation can be used to spark classroom discussions and encourage students to consider different perspectives. Writing prompts and learning activities that encourage students to take responsibility for their behavior and reflect on their actions can help to create a more accountable and supportive learning environment. And by using restorative circles and other practices, teachers can model positive communication and help students build a sense of community in the classroom. To reiterate these points, throughout the text we offer callout boxes like the following.

Throughout this book, you'll see callout boxes with this symbol, which represents the interconnectedness of UDL, social-emotional learning, character education, and restorative practices in the English language arts classroom. These frameworks are not standalone concepts but rather are woven together to create a comprehensive and inclusive approach to literacy instruction. The symbol will indicate specific examples of how each framework can be integrated into ELA instruction to create a more engaging and supportive learning environment. The purpose of this book is to ground our discussion of this work in ELA, even though it may seem like we're beating a dead horse. (C'mon, you love the idiom!) Listen, we know that sometimes it's good to repeat, replicate, and remind. (Rule of Three! We're on a roll!) So keep an eye out for the symbol and let it guide you on this journey to remind you what is uniquely fabulous about being an ELA teacher!

Note that this book is not a directive to build your own ELA curriculum, nor is it a call to revise every single unit or lesson. Rather, it's a way to think differently about implementing lessons as you create environments that foster academic excellence for all students by providing them with voice and choice.

Some of you may be reading this and thinking, *What if I already have a scripted curriculum that I have to use exactly as it is designed?* First of all, we hope, for your sake, that you don't have to teach a curriculum *exactly* as it's designed. High-quality instructional materials are an incredible resource to ensure all students have access to grade-level learning. That being said, as educators, you should have the autonomy to identify barriers within the curriculum and not replace, but rather supplement, the pathways so that all students can engage with the standards. When we work with teachers, we're like a broken record, saying, "You don't work for the curriculum. The curriculum works for you." You can still use a curriculum "with fidelity" and note barriers.

When you examine a text-based lesson, for example, you can predict that if you provide students with a printed text, some students may not yet decode at grade level, are multilingual learners who are not fluent in English yet, or have a visual impairment. To eliminate those barriers, you can provide the text digitally so students can use a read-aloud. You could also provide the option to translate the text or allow students to read with a partner or with you in a small group.

Additionally, you may choose to provide access to numerous poems and song lyrics or allow students to choose their own so they could compare and contrast the anchor text with a song of their choice. This will allow students to pair the text with one that connects to their interests.

Adopted curriculum often comes with comprehension questions for students to write responses. Examine whether the unit is explicitly focused on writing instruction. If it isn't, writing is "construct irrelevant," so consider offering the option for students to answer the questions in writing, in a video, or by discussing with classmates. You can even provide them with choices for discussion so they can become comfortable with multiple formats.

Remember that UDL lives in the "or," so provide the options. The firm goal is to comprehend the text and answer the questions to share that comprehension, and you can still do that with fidelity while providing students with options and choices to self-differentiate their pathways.

Regardless of whether you teach from an adopted curriculum or create your own lessons, this work is about viewing that curriculum through the lens of inclusive practices with team members to determine barriers and increase engagement to accelerate learning for all students.

Throughout the text, Jina, Brianne, Anne, Ryan, and I share specific strategies to build rich, collaborative, engaging literacy environments because we care deeply about our own literacy lives and the literary lives of our learners. As practitioners, we focus on multiple domains of literacy, including reading, writing, speaking, listening, and language and vocabulary development. When we discuss reading, however, we are focused on reading comprehension. We recognize the incredible value and necessity of learning to decode and the science of reading, but as secondary teachers, that is not our area of expertise.

We often interact with teachers who argue, "Kids have to read." When they say this, they are referring to foundational reading standards. We want our students to be able to decode text. We will never argue with that. However, there are some students who do not yet have those skills, and continuing to put inaccessible text in front of learners will exclude them from being able to access grade-level content. Since no one has a magical elixir to make a non-decoder a decoder instantly, we have a choice. We can either exclude a student, or we can implement UDL and include them. Once we are past the foundational reading standards, which conclude in grade 4, students need to have access to additional instruction in reading. These reading courses, or a remedial or recovery reading curriculum, need to be provided *in addition to*— not instead of—universally designed, grade-level instruction.

This book focuses on reading comprehension, writing, speaking, and listening. The practices can be used in classrooms preK–12, in college and careers, and in our professional learning lives as learners grapple, make sense of, and connect with the texts and artifacts around them. That being said, we acknowledge that these practices do not address foundational reading skills. That will be for another book. See what I did there? (;

Thank you for coming on this journey with us.

1

Integrating Practices to Support Your Why

Identifying Your Buttons

Jina Poirier

It's funny what we remember and what advice we choose to hold close to our hearts. I clearly recall some wisdom my master teacher, Mrs. Peterson, shared with me what seems like a lifetime ago: To be a successful teacher, I needed to keep two things in mind. First, I must identify my "buttons," or the things that get under my skin. Knowing your buttons, she argued, allows us to prepare our reactions when students unknowingly or knowingly push those buttons.

After 20 years in education, I can confidently say that when students know what makes us nuts, they don't quit! Suddenly they are committed to pushing that button over and over again. It's as though they're gaining extra credit for helping us practice our self-regulation skills. Bless their hearts!

In retrospect, this was incredible advice, considering my passion took me on a journey in alternative education. Maintaining our calm in chaotic situations is a prerequisite for working with at-promise youth or any teenagers. If we're being honest, remaining cool, calm, and collected in a staff meeting keeps us employed!

The second piece of advice from Mrs. Peterson was to know your "why." Made popular by Simon Sinek, an inspirational speaker and best-selling author of *Start With Why* (Sinek, 2009), the idea of starting with our why is all about recognizing our purpose. Sinek's Optimistic Company shares its mission, "We imagine a world in which the vast majority of people wake up every single morning inspired, feel safe wherever they are, and end the day fulfilled by the work they do." In hindsight, Mrs. Peterson was trying to set me on that path. She reminded me about my why.

Tapping into our why throughout our careers can be a strong anchor. My why is, and always will be, that I believe in students and that the right conditions and an excellent education can open pathways to allow them to be exactly who they want to be. Recently, I was inspired by a quote in Chris Emdin's book *Ratchet-demic*. Emdin (2021) writes, "It is about us taking a critical look at ourselves and how we have been shaped by institutions that rob us of our joy and passion while selling us a version of education that doesn't awaken the soul" (p. 11).

In my second year of college, deciding between becoming a social worker or a teacher was challenging. The one thing I knew was that I wanted a career where I could be a helper and lift others up along the way because I believe in people, the human spirit, and the ability to change the path of the people we serve. I am forever grateful to my Aunt Lynn for showing me that teaching is so much more than teaching content. It's about kids.

As teachers, we are counselors, bathroom monitors, lunch monitors, milk monitors, academic content instructors, instructional designers, role models, cleaners of noses, and sometimes even detectives. Experience shows us that no matter what setting we teach in, we need to know our students and build trusting relationships before we can focus on academics. Our job description may require expertise in English language arts, but we all know that learning doesn't occur until we're in an environment where we feel safe to fail and grow. So, let's add to the list.

In addition to the responsibilities just described, we are instructors who support academic learning, social-emotional learning, behavioral expectations, classroom community creation, character building, and restorative practices. We design instruction so that it is trauma-informed and linguistically appropriate. Wait— the standards don't tell us how to do that!! [cue breathing into a paper bag]

- How on earth are we supposed to do this all?
- Why do I need to wear so many different hats?
- Why must I continually build a skill set that evolves with every learner I meet?
- Why does it seem like there's no possible way to do all this?

All of these lead back to our purpose: to serve our kids. And we can do it all if there's an integration of inclusive practices in the very fiber of our classrooms. We've all worked in classrooms with students who need us to integrate these practices so that they can work toward mastery of academic standards. And believe us, it's effective. The five of us have very different experiences, but we've all seen firsthand how education can have an incredibly positive impact on the learners we serve when we get the conditions right.

Understanding Our Why

Understanding our why can be a powerful thing. Anne's three-year-old nephew, Emmett, is at the stage where he's always asking why.

Why does my favorite toy not work without batteries?

Why are there no more dinosaurs?

Why can't I have more cookies?

Answering "just because" is never enough. Kids are curious and want to know why something is happening or why things should be done a certain way. As we grow into adults, we ask why less and less, but maybe we shouldn't.

We are reminded of the age-old question inundating classrooms for generations: "Why do we have to learn this? I am never going to use it again in my life." Simply stating "because" is condescending and dismantles the relationship and trust between teacher and student. Students naturally want to know why, and we should challenge ourselves with the same questions daily.

The journey for us as educators is one of lifelong learning. To quote from one of the best films ever, "Goonies never say die!" (If you haven't seen *The Goonies*, pop some popcorn, find it on a streaming service, and enjoy the adventure, 1980s-style!) That said, our motto could be, "Teachers never stop learning!" Preparing the next generation for the future lives they want to live is a privilege we should not take lightly.

We are all inspired by the work of bell hooks (2014), whose essay "Engaged Pedagogy" speaks to our why:

> *To educate as the practice of freedom is a way of teaching that anyone can learn. That learning process comes easiest to those of us who teach who also believe that there is an aspect of our vocation that is sacred; who believe that our work is not merely to share information but to share in the intellectual and spiritual growth of our students. To teach in a manner that respects and cares for the souls of our students is essential if we are to provide the necessary conditions where learning can most deeply and intimately begin.*

Anyone can learn. However, to ensure that each and every one of our students learns at high levels, we have to adapt our practices, especially now. We live in a very interesting time in history.

In the last 100 years, the United States has changed tremendously. While our history has always illustrated growth and, at times, relapses, the changes of the last 100 years have been astronomical. Consider the differences between 1722 and 1822 and compare that to the differences between 1922 and 2022. The gains in science, technology, and medicine alone have been massive. Yet educational settings and methods of teaching, in large part, have failed to make the gains witnessed in other fields.

In the 2022 Nation's Report Card, in grades 4 and 8, reading levels continued to decrease. In 2019, both fourth and eighth graders dropped three points compared to 2017. In 2022, the National Center for Education Statistics (NCES) conducted a special administration of the NAEP long-term trend (LTT) reading assessment for nine-year-old students to examine student achievement during the COVID-19 pandemic. Average scores for these students in 2022 declined five points in reading compared to 2020. This is the largest average score decline in reading since 1990.

We recognize the limitations of standardized testing and that there are far more important ways to assess student learning. Still, declining student achievement on the tests, despite their many limitations, is not moving us in the right direction. This is especially true when we reflect on the words of bell hooks: "anyone can learn."

The definition of what it means to be literate has been an evolution. Traditional definitions of literacy focused on the ability to read and comprehend words, but now literacy is also considered a tool to participate more fully in the 21st century's digital society and transcends the English language arts class into all subject areas. Being able to read and understand texts, including multimedia texts, is now more important than ever (Tompkins, 2018). We all have digital lives, from social media to blogs to digital newspapers. We have instant access to literacy at the tips of our fingers with our smartphones. With the right texts, universal design, and accessible instruction, we can eliminate the barriers that make literacy a struggle and create expert, literate, confident learners.

Our view is how we can use the principles of UDL to make grade-level texts and literacy instruction accessible to all learners, regardless of variability, acknowledging that many secondary students with lagging decoding skills would benefit from additional support through multitiered systems. In short, we believe that all students should be able to enter a classroom with grade-level peers and have a teacher who says, regardless of the variability of the student, "You get to be exactly who you are, and I will support you to be wildly successful here."

To do this, we must embrace innovative technology and evidence-based, inclusive frameworks that put diverse students at the center of their learning experience. Companies like Microsoft 360 and Google Apps for Education (GAFE) have changed how we deliver content and provided us with tools for learners to self-differentiate their learning experience. Learning management systems like CANVAS, Blackboard, and Chalkboard provide a platform to engage students synchronously and asynchronously and provide accessibility tools that previously were not available. Also rocking the boat are maverick educators like Matt Miller, who has shared the ideas in his book *Ditch That Textbook* (2015) at keynotes around the globe, and Cornelius Minor, a literacy reformer and author of *We Got This* (2018), who calls on us to name, disrupt, and dismantle barriers in education.

Despite advances in technology and innovation, too many students from resilient communities are not included in general education classrooms with their peers; fail to make academic progress; experience poor outcomes socially, emotionally, and behaviorally; and do not feel they belong in the classrooms that serve them. When focused specifically on English language arts, too many students don't have access to grade-level texts, aren't interested in the texts they are assigned, and don't see the purpose of literacy in their lives (Hinkle, Parker, Reed, & Wolff, 2019). They don't recognize the power of language to craft authentic messages to write or speak their truth. Troubling statistics concerning literacy in our current youth culture are not only staggering but downright frightening. It has been well documented that having a reading level far below grade level correlates with higher school dropout rates, failure to attend college, and an increased risk of living in poverty, serving time in jail, and having a shorter life span (Buffam, Mattos, & Weber, 2010).

You, like us, have probably received professional development on the following frameworks in the past few years: UDL, social-emotional learning, character development, and restorative practices (Figure 1-1). If you think of each of these frameworks as isolated, your head will spin. You may wonder how to divide up your literacy block or your English language arts class so you have a time slot for all of them. The truth? You will run out of time.

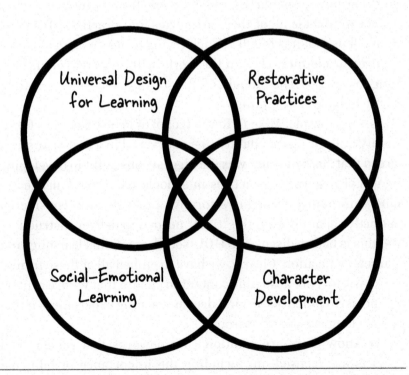

Figure 1-1. Intersection of four frameworks to strengthen ELA instruction

As practitioners, we have all been in your shoes. We know that you can't get blood from a stone, though William Wallace (aka Braveheart) certainly tried. We all felt we were underwater, and it didn't seem like an end was in sight. Alas, over mini tacos at a retirement luncheon, inspiration hit the A-Team. They recognized that there was a way to do it all, but they had to integrate it. Just as their taco shells were filled with proteins, cheeses, and veggies, the team realized their literacy blocks needed to mix academic content, social-emotional learning, character education, and restorative practices.

We all know the feeling, the spark, the reason we went into education so many years ago. Or maybe the mini tacos were the brain food needed for inspiration. Who doesn't love tacos? And if you don't, take that to the grave.

Don't worry. We already know what you're thinking. The typical argument is that there isn't enough time in the day for a teacher to include all of these strategies and practices. Teachers often tell us that it is tough enough trying to get through all of the required academics. How in the world will they add yet another thing to the day? The thought of integrating even a single framework can be overwhelming.

As one example, Mike D. Revell (2020) of Prince George's Community College shares that teachers surveyed in a two-year study agreed that "lack of time" was the biggest constraint to developing the use of restorative practices in schools. The "time" needed to build community through restorative practices was considered distinctly separate from the "time" needed to deliver instruction. And this is before discussing UDL, social-emotional learning, and character education. Clearly, we have to embed all of these frameworks within core academic content to ensure that we are centering inclusive practices around deeper learning experiences in the English language arts classroom.

We know there are additional frameworks that schools and districts are focused on, including the importance of bilingual education, trauma-informed instruction, culturally responsive pedagogy, project-based learning, and blended learning, among others. Our focus on UDL, social-emotional learning, character education, and restorative practices is not intended to prioritize these frameworks over the others. Rather, we have extensive experience and expertise in those four areas and want to share our success in integrating them and the impact it has had on countless students we have served.

 English language arts teachers have a unique privilege that other teachers may envy: the opportunity to engage with students on an intimate level through the written and spoken word. Language is the foundation of learning. It is the medium through which we communicate ideas, build relationships, and make meaning of the world around us. Focusing on the four domains of literacy—reading, writing, speaking, and listening—is essential to developing strong language skills, which are crucial to success in all areas of life.

Secondly, when learners feel safe and supported in their learning environment, they are more likely to take risks, make mistakes, and embrace new challenges. This is particularly important when it comes to literacy, where learners may feel vulnerable or self-conscious about their skills. By creating a safe and inclusive space where learners can develop their language skills in all four domains, educators can help learners build confidence, resilience, and a lifelong love of learning.

Finally, it's worth noting that the four domains of literacy are deeply interconnected, just as the frameworks we discuss throughout this text. Reading, writing, speaking, and listening are not isolated skills, but rather build upon and reinforce one another. For example, reading and writing are intimately connected—the ability to read fluently and critically is essential to effective writing, while writing can help learners clarify their thinking and deepen their understanding of what they have read. Similarly, speaking and listening are integral to effective communication, both inside and outside the classroom.

We have the power to help our students discover their voices, explore their identities, and make sense of the world around them. We have been humbled and honored to support our learners in using the frameworks integrated throughout this book to write arguments about things they care about, debate issues of importance, develop their writing voices, and share their hearts through poetry. We have windows and pathways to the hearts and minds of our students and their emotions, and we can weave this knowledge naturally into the fabric of the standards we are required to teach.

Reflection Questions

1. Take a minute and think about your why. Why did you choose education as your career? Discuss your answer with a friend or colleague, write a blog or poem, or create a multimedia product to remind you of your why.

2. This book will focus on teaching inclusive English language arts classrooms with a focus on grade-level instruction, UDL, social-emotional learning, character education, and restorative practices. What is your familiarity with these frameworks in your own practice?

3. Integrating evidence-based frameworks is imperative if we want to meet the needs of all learners. Consider how you currently integrate multiple frameworks into your literacy instruction. Share with colleagues by writing a blog or sharing your learning with a multimedia artifact. Consider making a podcast, recording a vlog, or making an infographic. And please share it with us!

2

Unpacking and Connecting Frameworks

I Love the Look of Words

Popcorn leaps, popping from the floor
of a hot black skillet and into my mouth.
Black words leap,
snapping from the white
page. Rushing into my eyes. Sliding
into my brain which gobbles them
the way my tongue and teeth
chomp the buttered popcorn.

When I have stopped reading,
ideas from the words stay stuck
in my mind, like the sweet
smell of butter perfuming my
fingers long after the popcorn
is finished.
I love the book and the look of words
the weight of ideas that popped into my mind.
I love the tracks
Of new thinking of my mind.

—Maya Angelou

In classrooms from preK to higher education, students in English language arts classrooms examine and closely read poetry. Instruction often begins by sharing a poem with students. Maybe the text is printed in an anthology or on a handout so students can annotate. Sometimes teachers project the poem and read it aloud to students, encouraging them to read it with feeling and fluency. After appreciating the poem, students discuss and then respond to it in writing. Younger learners may use a combination of writing, drawing, and dictating to respond to the poem or draft their own. Older students may answer multiple-choice questions about the author's tone, use of figurative language, and meaning.

For example, after reading "I Love the Look of Words," students may respond to the prompt, "What is Maya Angelou's message about the power and beauty of words? Use evidence from the text to support your answer."

Most likely, we've all used a lesson like this. Take a moment to think about a poetry lesson that you teach. In this chapter, we'll introduce UDL, social-emotional learning, character education, and restorative practices by describing how a poetry lesson can be transformed to integrate all of the frameworks to create classrooms that are rigorous, nurturing, and flexible.

Universal Design for Learning

If you're reading this book, it's likely because you or your school, district, or education prep program is interested in UDL. Either way, we're so happy you're here. *UDL Now!* (Novak, 2022) defines UDL by these beliefs and values, which guide the UDL practitioner's work:

- ⮞ Variability is the rule, not the exception. Individual learners may need to learn differently, using different materials, to reach the same goals.

- ⮞ All students can work toward the same firm goals and grade-level standards when provided with conditions of nurture and adequate support.

- ⮞ All learners can become expert learners if barriers are removed (Meyer, Rose, & Gordon, 2014).

These beliefs must lead the way as you transform your classroom to better meet the needs of your learners. Educators often hear about UDL and think of it as a checklist of skills and strategies. But skills and strategies alone won't result in the change necessary to create a more inclusive, equitable classroom if they're not rooted in the belief that all students can be supported to comprehend complex texts, contribute to rich classroom discussions, and share their learning in authentic ways.

The book *Equity by Design: Delivering on the Promise and Power of UDL* (Chardin & Novak, 2020) argues that to have equity in education, all students, regardless of identity, must have the following:

- Equitable access to inclusive classrooms with grade-level peers
- Equitable opportunities to learn aligned to grade-level standards
- Equitable expectations that they can be successful when provided with the appropriate support
- Equitable feelings of belonging and hope

To get there, you need to design for it by incorporating the UDL principles: multiple means of engagement, multiple means of representation, and multiple means of action and expression.

Provide multiple means of engagement. Engagement is at the core of all learning experiences. If we want students to learn, we must foster both attention and commitment by providing students with authentic, meaningful experiences in learning. All students need access to options that help them connect their own strengths to new learning activities, as well as access to their peers to foster collaboration and community.

Provide multiple means of representation. Not all learners comprehend information in the same way, have the same background information, or have access to the same vocabulary.

You must offer multiple access and entry points so that all students can grow as learners toward the same goals. By providing multiple opportunities and options for students to learn information, you empower them to personalize how they build knowledge and skills.

Provide multiple means of action and expression. It is not enough to comprehend information if there is no way to express it. Students need numerous methods to express their understanding as they develop into writers and speakers in ways that are developmentally appropriate for them and that embrace emerging technologies.

You can operationalize the UDL principles by recognizing four curriculum components that make up a complete learning experience. Regardless of your lesson planning format or process, all lesson plans consider goals, methods, materials, and assessments. Table 2-1 highlights the four core components of curriculum and describes each component through the UDL lens.

Table 2-1. Considerations for UDL Lesson Design

	UDL definition	Considerations	Reflection questions
Goals	All UDL lessons start with a clear learning goal based on state standards or district proficiencies. Goals include verbs that foster multiple means of action and expression.	Instead of, "Students will write an argument essay," revise to "Students will write an argument," which is the language of the standard. This allows choices and options for essays, letters, speeches, and the like.	★ What are your firm goals? ★ Do they connect explicitly to grade-level standards? ★ Do your goals allow for multiple means of representation and/or action and expression?

Table 2-1 Continued. Considerations for UDL Lesson Design

	UDL definition	Considerations	Reflection questions
Assessment	Assessments gather information about a learner's performance. Often, we think of these as "tests," but they can be any expression of knowledge that allows the educator to determine a student's progress toward mastery of the goal.	Examine each goal and consider whether there is more than one way to reach it. List all the ways students could potentially "show" that they met the goal. It's important to create a rubric that would assess all options.	★ Throughout the unit, is there an opportunity for diagnostic, formative, and summative assessments? ★ Do students have a choice about how to express their learning as they all work toward firm goals, especially in diagnostic and formative assessments?
Methods	There are multiple ways students can learn content, build background information, and explore the knowledge and skills under study. In UDL, students can choose which methods they will use to learn.	Instead of lecturing to all students and then requiring the whole class to watch a video, revise to, "After a mini-lesson, students will choose to participate in small-group instruction, watch a video on Google Classroom, read a chapter in the course text, or listen to an audio version of the text." Know there is always more than one way for students to learn.	★ Do students have a choice about how they will build knowledge and access resources?

Table 2-1 Continued. Considerations for UDL Lesson Design

	UDL definition	Considerations	Reflection questions
Materials	Materials are the resources used to present learning content and what the learner uses to demonstrate knowledge.	Set up a buffet of resources for students to choose from. Offer graphic organizers, Chromebooks, exemplars, and more. Don't require all students to use the same materials to learn and express what they know. Because of variability, they won't all need the same support, and they should be empowered to know themselves as learners and choose what they need.	★ Do students have a choice about the materials they will use to learn or complete the assessment?

Because UDL is a standards-based curriculum design, we must start with how to establish firm goals. If possible, have your ELA standards in front of you because this process is easier if they're accessible. As you read your standards, you'll notice that some of them require students to have specific knowledge, while others require them to build specific skills. This is the difference between content standards and method standards (those with specific tasks or means embedded). The difference between the two types of standards needs to be understood because each type lends itself to different UDL strategies.

The level of choice you provide in your methods, materials, and assessments will be determined by the standard. Next time you find yourself reviewing a standard, don't jump to a quick conclusion about how your traditional assessment is the only way to measure progress. Instead, ask yourself, "Is there any other way my students could show me they have met this standard?" Sometimes the answer will be no, but more often than not, the answer is yes.

If all students have to produce writing, which is a critical skill, we aren't going to provide options for them to record an audio clip. Rather, we need to identify the barriers that prevent high-quality writing. For example, some students struggle with fine motor skills, organization, or knowing what to write about. Once we are clear that writing is the goal, we can provide students with the option to write, type, or use voice to text. We can provide options for examining multiple exemplars of high-quality writing through reading or listening. We can provide graphic organizers, checklists, and options for writing conferences.

The UDL principles and the UDL design process require educators to ask three core questions:

1. What is it that all learners need to know or be able to do?
2. Based on variability, what barriers may prevent students from learning or sharing what they know?
3. How do I design flexible pathways using the principles of UDL so all learners can learn and share what they know?

Let's examine those three questions (Table 2-2) as they relate to a poetry lesson on "I Love the Look of Words" using the guidance from the considerations in Table 2-1.

Table 2-2. UDL Reflection: "I Love the Look of Words"

UDL core question	Response
What is it that all learners need to know or be able to do?	Imagine the focus of this unit is that students will learn more about theme and will be able to identify themes while citing textual evidence. This aligns with the following anchor standards: ★ Read closely to determine what the text says explicitly and to make logical inferences; cite specific textual evidence when writing or speaking to support conclusions drawn from the text. ★ Determine central ideas or themes of a text and analyze their development; summarize the key supporting details and ideas. These standards are reading comprehension standards, not foundation reading standards, so it is critical that all students access the text.
Based on variability, what barriers may prevent students from learning or sharing what they know?	Barriers include learners not being able to decode the text, multilingual learners not being able to access the text in English, and students not having the background knowledge about what popcorn looks like when it pops from a skillet (we blame microwave popcorn!) to understand the text. If students are asked to write a response, that can create a barrier, given that the standard notes the importance of citing evidence when writing or speaking. Since writing is not one of the identified standards, writing may present a barrier for students who struggle with written language.
How do I design flexible pathways using the principles of UDL so all learners can learn and share what they know?	Before reading, the teacher can show videos of popcorn popping from a skillet to address barriers with background knowledge. Students can access the text in a hard copy so they can annotate, or they can access it digitally so they can access translation tools, read-aloud tools, and the like. Additionally, they can have the option to listen to the text in a small group. When responding to the prompt, they could have access to a printed or digital graphic organizer to plan and then share the answer to the question in writing, by making a video or audio or sharing their response using multimedia like an infographic or slide deck.

Note that in this lesson, students are given numerous choices about their learning. Extensive research shows that giving students choices increases engagement, motivation, persistence, and buy-in. It also shows that students spend more time and effort on their learning tasks when offered choices and that having choices helps them build other important skills, such as self-regulation (Patall, Cooper, & Wynn, 2010). That being said, we have to be careful not to overwhelm students with choices.

Providing too much choice creates a barrier. Barry Schwartz (2005), the author of *Paradox of Choice* and the speaker of a popular TED Talk by the same name, says in his talk, "One effect, paradoxically, is that [providing choice] produces paralysis rather than liberation. With so many options to choose from, people find it very difficult to choose at all." Furthermore, "If one manages to overcome paralysis and choose, evidence suggests that the quality of performance deteriorates with increases in the number of options." This choice paralysis and decreased performance can be minimized through design.

At this point, you're likely asking, "How much choice is too much?" Research has an answer for you: seven. Seven is too much. Choice paralysis and dissatisfaction increase exponentially after "a limited array of 6 choices" (Iyengar & Lepper, 2000). That doesn't mean that six is the magic number, but six is the maximum number of choices that you can offer before you are dangerously close to choice paralysis. Additional research suggests that two to four choices is the sweet spot (Patall, Cooper, & Robinson, 2008).

In our UDL poetry lesson, we addressed predictable academic barriers that may prevent learning by providing strategic options and choices, but as you know, students face many barriers that prevent them from accessing academics, even those that are flexibly designed. These barriers, whether social, emotional, or behavioral, must also be addressed through design. This is where it's important to recognize that we can eliminate barriers, thereby universally designing our classrooms by incorporating additional frameworks like social-emotional learning, character education, and restorative practices.

Social-Emotional Learning

Social-emotional learning (SEL) is in full force among educators today. As it should be! Even prior to experiencing a global pandemic, focusing on SEL made perfect sense. The pandemic only amplified the need for our students to have strategies to better understand and navigate emotions, conflicts, and relationships. The Collaborative for Academic, Social, and Emotional Learning (CASEL) argues that SEL helps learners acquire and effectively apply the knowledge, attitudes, and skills necessary to understand and manage emotions, set and achieve positive goals, feel and show empathy for others, establish and maintain positive relationships, and make responsible decisions. The ability to identify what you are feeling and adjust according to your needs is a valuable skill in living a healthy life, and research is clear that social-emotional learning has considerable benefits to learners.

In a meta-analysis of 213 studies involving more than 270,000 students, Durlak, Weissberg, Dymnicki, Taylor, and Schellinger (2011) found that SEL interventions increased students' academic performance by 11 percentile points and that students participating in SEL programs showed improved classroom behavior, an increased ability to manage stress and depression, and better attitudes about themselves, others, and school.

K. C. Knudson (2022), a UDL consultant and one of Katie's amazing colleagues, does a tremendous job of unpacking social-emotional learning and its impact on our instructional practices. He notes:

> *In my experience and my research, I find that SEL is inclusive of three critical bodies of work: Social Emotional Conditions (SEC)—the feeling of belonging and acceptance within a place; the sensation of being authentically valued as a whole person*

> *and a genuine participant; Social Emotional Skills (SES)—the interpersonal and intrapersonal skills that support our effective function within a community of people; the self-regulation and social skills identified by organizations like CASEL; and finally, Social Emotional Academic Development (SEAD)—the neuro-scientific research that confirms that all learning is socially and emotionally constructed; the research that says we must tend to learner emotions and provide opportunities for social sense-making if we want students to learn anything at all.*

In Table 2-3, we unpack the three prongs of social-emotional learning. As you read, consider instructional practices in your own learning environment that align with each prong.

Table 2-3. The Three Prongs of Social-Emotional Learning (Adapted From Knudson, 2022)

Prong	Description
Social-emotional conditions (SEC)	The social-emotional conditions of a school setting are often defined as the culture and climate of a school setting and their impact on students' level of engagement, achievement, and well-being. Many studies indicate that there is a connection between a student's sense of belonging, sense of well-being, and academic achievement.
Social-emotional skills (SES)	CASEL forwards five critical nonacademic skills that need to be developed in our students: self-awareness, self-management, social awareness, relationship skills, and responsible decision-making. Many states have taken these competencies and created their own SEL proficiencies as required learning targets.
Social-emotional academic development (SEAD)	Social-emotional academic development is described in the recent book *How People Learn II* by the National Academies of Sciences, Engineering, and Medicine (2018). Their review of scientific research notes that individuals' brains are shaped by social relationships, and the information they learn through these relationships supports both their emotions and their learning.

If we are clear in our understanding that SEL incorporates SEC, SES, and SEAD, then we can be more clear in our efforts to improve learning environments and learning for all students. One way to operationalize social-emotional learning is to use CASEL's 3 Signature Practices (CASEL, 2019):

- **A welcoming/inclusion activity or routine** that builds community and connects to the work ahead. For example, one recommended activity is called *Synectics*, or projecting an image on a screen while learners complete a sentence stem, such as "[Given topic] is like this [image] because . . . ." Participants generate and record as many comparisons as possible between the image displayed and the topic presented in one to two minutes.

- **Engagement strategies** throughout the learning experience that offer many opportunities of varying complexity to practice SEL skills. Engagement strategies include opportunities for students to turn and talk, think-pair-share, have private think time, and take brain breaks. Build a balance of interactive and reflective experiences to meet the needs of all participants.

- An **optimistic closure** that highlights an individual and shared understanding of the importance of the work and can provide a sense of reflection and accomplishment. One example of an optimistic closure is an activity called "Suit Yourself" (see the following box), which uses playing cards to prompt reflection.

Suit Yourself

 "Suit Yourself" (CASEL, 2019, p. 45) builds responsible decision-making skills (reflection, evaluation) as participants are asked to identify how engagement impacted them. It opens the group to social awareness skill development as they notice how much individual takeaways vary (perspective-taking, empathy, appreciating diversity) from the same experience.

1. Randomly pass out a playing card to each participant. Each suit describes a category of responses:

    ☀ **Hearts:** Something from the heart. How did you feel? What did it mean to you?

    ☀ **Clubs:** Things that grew—new ideas, new thoughts, a new point of view.

    ☀ **Diamonds:** Gems that last forever. What are some of the gems of wisdom gathered from people or content?

    ☀ **Spades:** Used to dig in the garden. Generate conversation about planting new ideas or things participants dug up during class.

2. Give one minute of quiet time for each participant to jot down (or think about) their answer.

3. Debrief using one of the following:

    ☀ Ask for one volunteer from each suit to share their response. Do not comment during the sharing.

    ☀ Ask participants to turn to a neighbor and share their response.

    ☀ Invite each participant to answer aloud to you as they walk out the door or hand in their written response as an exit ticket.

Let's take our UDL poetry lesson and incorporate SEL using CASEL's 3 Signature Practices into the instructional methods. See Table 2-4.

Table 2-4. UDL Poetry Lesson With 3 Signature Practices

Curriculum component	UDL considerations
Goals	★ Read closely to determine what the text says explicitly and to make logical inferences; cite specific textual evidence when writing or speaking to support conclusions drawn from the text. ★ Determine central ideas or themes of a text and analyze their development; summarize the key supporting details and ideas.
Methods	★ **Welcoming activity.** Synectics: Display an image of popcorn popping on a skillet. Provide the sentence stem, "Popcorn is like reading because . . ." and provide a minute for private think time before sharing. ★ **Mini-lesson.** Give a 10-minute lesson on close reading with a particular focus on visualizing and providing time for students to choose their learning paths. ★ **Self-differentiated learning.** Students will access "I Love the Look of Words" in hard copy or digitally and will read closely alone, with a partner, or in a small group before participating in a discussion of Maya Angelou's message about the power and beauty of words. Encourage a five-minute brain break halfway through the class period. ★ **Optimistic closure.** Use "Suit Yourself" to reflect on what students learned about their learning process by making choices throughout the lesson.
Materials	★ Printed and digital copies of the poem "I Love the Look of Words." ★ 1:1 devices ★ Graphic organizers to organize response ★ Assessment rubric
Assessment	Students will have a choice board for how they choose to answer the question, "What is Maya Angelou's message about the power and beauty of words in 'I Love the Look of Words'?" using textual evidence. There will be an option to revise after receiving feedback. The choice board will include the option to write a response (on paper or digitally), record audio or video, and/or create a multimedia response.

Character Education

As any experienced educator can attest, not only do we instruct on our content area and focus on social-emotional learning, we have the added benefit of coaching and guiding our students on being all-around good people. As teachers, we are destined not just to teach the standards, frameworks, and roadmaps of the curriculum but also to prepare students for their future lives. Most of us can understand the value of infusing character education into the curriculum, as it seems almost as obvious as teaching students to read and write. Character education typically aims to develop traits such as:

- **Respect:** Valuing oneself and others, including diverse groups and opinions
- **Responsibility:** Showing commitment to one's actions, decisions, and obligations
- **Kindness:** Demonstrating compassion and care for others
- **Fairness:** Treating others justly and impartially
- **Courage:** Standing up for one's beliefs and facing challenges
- **Perseverance:** Showing persistence in pursuing goals despite obstacles
- **Self-regulation:** Controlling one's own thoughts, feelings, and actions

Note that these character traits look familiar—they're often identified as a school or district's core values or articulated in a portrait of a learner. There are clear connections with social-emotional learning, but the two frameworks are not the same. While SEL is focused on building self-awareness, social awareness, responsible decision-making, and strong relationships, character education is focused on helping students embody core values. And as students become more self-aware of their character, the hope is that they will make responsible decisions to better represent those values in their lives.

In the book *UDL Playbook for School and District Leaders*, Katie and Mike Woodlock (2022) discuss the importance of core values and provide the following prompts to begin conversations about them:

- ➲ Which of our core values is our school community in need of the most?

- ➲ How would we embody these core values through our practice?

- ➲ How would we recognize these core values when we see them in our classrooms?

Using these prompts with colleagues and with students can help highlight the importance of your core values so that you can provide explicit instruction and framing that incorporate those values, supporting students in building their identity as learners in addition to their character as humans.

Given our UDL/SEL poetry lesson, it would be easy to incorporate a focus on respect, perseverance, or self-discipline. As an example, the welcoming activity asked students to make connections between an image of popcorn and reading. Before students respond, you could take a moment to discuss the importance of being respectful of other people's ideas, even if they seem inaccurate, strange, or off base. Because we all have different backgrounds, thoughts, feelings, and experiences, we may have some very different interpretations of the analogy. A reminder about what respect looks like by prompting students with, "How can we embody respect as we share our ideas?" is a great way to incorporate character education while also supporting social-emotional skills.

Restorative Practices

Restorative practices aim to build a learning community where everyone is seen, heard, and welcomed regardless of their identity, ability, and lived experiences. It is human nature to want to be seen and feel heard. It can also be one of the most challenging tasks for a classroom teacher. The reality is that we have multiple class periods each day with up to 30 to 40 students on our rosters each period. In order to build relationships with this many students, teachers need superhero strength. How can we eliminate the barriers so that *all* students feel seen and heard and are involved in designing how they learn? Lean into restorative practices as your tool for building and sustaining relationships and community.

Mirko Chardin, Chief Equity Officer at Novak Educational Consulting, and colleague Edgar Vasquez share the power and purpose of restorative practices in our work:

> *If we truly value our students, then we have to be willing to institute circle/restorative practice structures to enhance and develop them to become their best selves while fostering social and emotional competencies. We want to effectively communicate to students that their voice is important and that it matters. We must emphasize that we will hear their voices on what they need, but that we will also make efforts to respond to and incorporate their feedback into our practice, school, and classroom communities by showing that their voice has value. When students are at the center and are engaged in discourse, they develop agency and an active role in the process which results in a willingness to commit with a seriousness of purpose (Chardin & Vasquez, 2022).*

Although it may seem like a leap to integrate restorative practices, you may actually have one foot in the door. If you've ever engaged in any of the following, then, believe it or not, you've experienced restorative practice:

- ➲ Expressed to a young person how their actions made you feel ("I'm so proud of you for ... !" or "I was really disappointed when ... ")

- Asked a young person how something impacted them, either negatively or positively

- Asked a young person to think about the impact of their actions after they were involved in some type of conflict

- Observed two young people get into a conflict with each other, pulled them aside, asked them what happened, and helped them discuss the situation and apologize to each other

- Sat in a circle with a group of people and had everyone go around and respond to a check-in question

- Held a meeting between a student and a staff member to work to resolve an incident that occurred between them (Chardin & Chu-Sheriff, forthcoming 2023)

One way to operationalize restorative practices in your ELA class is by using circle practice. Boyles-Watson and Pranis (2000), authors of *Circle Forward: Building a Restorative School Community*, define a circle as a carefully constructed, intentional dialogue space that supplements, not detracts from, academic instruction.

 Restorative practices can have a tremendous impact on creating a safe and inclusive classroom community in the English language arts classroom. When students feel comfortable and supported in their learning environment, they are more likely to engage with the curriculum and each other. Restorative practices can be particularly valuable in the ELA classroom because of the emphasis on communication and collaboration. Incorporating regular restorative circle practice can help build a strong and supportive classroom community by creating opportunities for students to connect with one another on a deeper level. Circles can be used as an opening or closing activity or even integrated into a lesson as a way to deepen understanding of a particular text or theme. When students participate in restorative circles regularly, they develop a sense of trust and respect for one another, creating a safe and supportive space for learning and growth.

Additionally, ELA instruction often involves group work, classroom discussions, and opportunities for students to share their ideas and perspectives with their peers. When conflicts arise in these situations, it is important to have a framework for addressing them that promotes constructive dialogue and understanding. Restorative practices can help students learn how to listen actively, express themselves effectively, and work together to find mutually beneficial solutions to conflicts. By providing students with these skills, teachers can create a more inclusive and supportive classroom community that fosters academic success and personal growth for all students, particularly at-promise youth.

Some schools have enacted restorative practices as a separate entity from their curriculum, which is problematic, especially when you consider how crucial a classroom community is for learning at high levels. In Pittsburgh Public Schools, academic achievement, especially with African American students, fell when restorative practices were implemented. While research is inconclusive at this point, "one explanation for the uneven test results might simply be that teachers diverted time from academics, causing students to be less prepared for exams" (Barnum, 2019). Cristine Cray, an official at Pittsburgh Public Schools, wants "teachers to see how restorative practices can be used to complement academic instruction and not replace academic instruction."

For example, think of the discussions that you can support in the classroom before you prepare to closely read a text. In the example in this chapter, we are designing a lesson on "I Love the

Look of Words." As a character education activity, we suggested prompting students with the question, "How can we embody respect as we share our ideas?" This could be used as a circle prompt, which increases engagement and also helps form that bond and community within your room that are the hallmarks of a successful restorative practices environment. A circle could also be used as an optimistic closure using the "Suit Yourself" activity (p. 32). If we can create a classroom community where students choose to share in restorative circles, we can see them as they see themselves, as they truly are.

This chapter has highlighted how you can take a traditional lesson, using a high-quality text, and incorporate UDL, SEL, character education, and restorative practices. At the beginning of this chapter, we imagined a class receiving a hard copy of the poem and being asked to write a response. Take a moment and consider the graphic organizer in Table 2-5, which incorporates all the frameworks discussed in this chapter, and how many more students would have relevant, authentic, and meaningful opportunities to participate in a supportive classroom community while accessing grade-level instruction.

Table 2-5. UDL Poetry Lesson With SEL, Character Education, and Restorative Practices

Component	Revisions
Goals	★ Read closely to determine what the text says explicitly and to make logical inferences; cite specific textual evidence when writing or speaking to support conclusions drawn from the text. ★ Determine central ideas or themes of a text and analyze their development; summarize the key supporting details and ideas.

Table 2-5 Continued. UDL Poetry Lesson With SEL, Character Education, and Restorative Practices

Component	Revisions
Methods	★ **Welcoming activity.** Open class with a circle. Discuss what respect looks like in the first circle round. Next, display an image of popcorn popping on a skillet. Provide the sentence stem, "Popcorn is like reading because . . . " and provide a minute for private think time before facilitating a circle process where they share and listen in a respectful way.
	★ **Mini-lesson.** Give a 10-minute lesson on close reading with a particular focus on visualizing, framing options, and providing time for students to choose their learning paths. Prompt them to share their paths and be respectful listeners.
	★ **Self-differentiated learning.** Students will access "I Love the Look of Words" and read closely alone, with a partner, or in a small group; will have options for discussion; and then will independently complete the assessment. Encourage five-minute brain breaks halfway through the class period.
	★ **Optimistic closure.** Close with a circle using "Suit Yourself" to reflect on what they learned about their learning process by making choices throughout the lesson.
Materials	★ Printed and digital copies of the poem "I Love the Look of Words."
	★ 1:1 devices
	★ Graphic organizers to organize response
	★ Assessment rubric
Assessment	Students will have a choice board for how they choose to answer the question, "What is Maya Angelou's message about the power and beauty of words in 'I Love the Look of Words'?" using textual evidence. There will be an option to revise after receiving feedback. The choice board will include the option to write a response (on paper or digitally), record audio or video, and/or create a multimedia response.

We think of academic instruction, UDL, social-emotional learning, character education, and restorative practices as productive partners, comrades that work in unison to achieve the ultimate goal for our students: an effective educational environment that provides safe, equitable, and accessible learning opportunities for all students, especially those students who benefit most from the integration of the frameworks.

Reflection Questions

1. We discussed UDL, SEL, character education, and restorative practices in this chapter as frameworks to proactively eliminate barriers that prevent all students from learning at high levels. What proactive strategies do you intentionally use to promote equity, access, and inclusion?

2. In this chapter, we revised a poetry lesson using UDL, SEL, character education, and restorative practices. As you imagine a lesson in your own course, how could you begin to incorporate the frameworks in your own class?

3. Consider the "before" lesson and the "after" lesson. How would the revised lesson increase access and engagement for all learners?

3

The Power of PLCs

Toppling Jenga

Katie Novak

By now, you may be thinking, *There is NO way I can do this by myself!* I felt a little like that the first time I met my co-authors. When I saw their curriculum, I imagined myself again as a secondary English teacher with my scope and sequence already bursting at the seams, and then I started to imagine piling everything else on top of it. With 42-minute classes, no less!

In my head, all I could envision was that giant lawn-sized version of Jenga (you know, the ones they have at outdoor restaurants and breweries), and I could feel the splintered boards slamming into my head as I stretched on my tiptoes to balance one more 2×4 on top. Oh, maybe that's a little dramatic, but I imagine I'm in good company. ELA teachers love their hyperboles!

Here's the thing: You should not be doing this alone. Even if you're a singleton in your school or district, you need to find your people and create a professional learning community (PLC), because let's face it: There are way too many people replicating the same work. The more we band together, the more time we have to ourselves. In this chapter, we'll discuss the importance of PLCs in supporting this integrated work.

In the third edition of *UDL Now!*, Chapter 1 is aptly called "Don't Do It Alone," which reminds us that there is so much power in collective efficacy. Forming a community of educators who work on implementing UDL together is critical for success. We need support, resources, and opportunities to collaborate so we can learn together, lean on one another, and celebrate our successes. We've all heard the saying, "Teamwork makes the dream work." As cheesy as it sounds, it's true. When you work on a project by yourself, you are limiting the project's potential. Working with a team allows you to bounce ideas off of each other, and ultimately you'll end up with a much better product.

My co-authors are well aware that the integrative design of UDL, SEL, restorative practices, and character education would not exist without the unique traits that each person brings to the project. Jina, Brianne, Anne, and Ryan brought different skill sets, backgrounds, and experiences to the group. You can bring the same expertise to your PLC by collaborating with ELA teachers with different strengths, as well as special educators, ELL support teachers, library media specialists, and adjustment counselors. Be inclusive!

An Inclusive PLC

Some of you may already have a PLC scheduled by the school, but think bigger. The more diverse and creative the team, the more students we can reach, which in the end will benefit students. If you're struggling to implement social-emotional learning, invite a school adjustment counselor to your team. Looking to better support students who have complex support needs? Invite a special educator. Also, welcome cognitive dissonance as you work with one another. Conflict and disagreements elicit innovative dialogue and are an integral part of the PLC process. As educators, we are often taught so fervently to respect one another that we fail to grasp the importance and necessity of conflict and disagreements.

A PLC can be the absolute best approach to this work because it helps us to build a team and focus on student outcomes. If you aren't familiar with what a PLC is, it's important to clarify that it isn't just a different name for a faculty meeting or a co-planning group. In their article "The Futility of PLC Lite," DuFour and Reeves (2016) argue that PLCs often fail to change teacher practice or increase student achievement because they don't focus on curriculum design or evidence-based decision-making. The authors note that in meaningful PLCs, teachers grapple with four core questions:

- ➲ What do we want students to learn?
- ➲ How will we know if they have learned it?
- ➲ What will we do if they have not learned it?
- ➲ How will we provide extended learning opportunities for students who have mastered the content?

These questions build collective efficacy when teachers have shared goals about student outcomes and purposeful time to address these questions as they share their unique expertise. By thoughtfully considering these questions, your PLC can fully embrace the central tenets of the PLC process and create an environment that fosters higher levels of learning for both students and adults (DuFour & Reeves, 2016). Table 3-1 examines the core questions of PLCs through the lens of UDL. As you reflect on these considerations, you may want to take notes using the following prompts:

- ➲ What do you notice?
- ➲ What do you wonder?

Table 3-1. PLC Questions With UDL Considerations (Novak, 2022)

PLC core questions	UDL considerations
What do we want all students to know and be able to do?	How does this step align with understanding "firm goals" and grade-level standards, a core component of UDL to ensure that all students—especially those students who have been historically underserved, marginalized, and minoritized—have access to advanced coursework?
How will we know if they learn it?	How can we design inclusive assessments that are equitable, aligned to firm goals/grade-level standards, and culturally responsive?
How will we respond when some students do not learn?	Which barriers can we eliminate through design? Be sure to explicitly examine access and engagement as well as barriers that prevent access because curriculum and instruction are not trauma-informed, linguistically appropriate, and culturally sustaining.
How will we extend the learning for students who are already proficient?	What are potential barriers to deep engagement and acceleration?

John Hattie is a professor of education and director of the Melbourne Education Research Institute at the University of Melbourne, Australia. Hattie developed a way of synthesizing various influences in different meta-analyses according to their effect size on student learning. He ranks 252 influences and their effect sizes related to student achievement. In this ranking system, the number one best indicator of student achievement is collective teaching efficacy, which he defines as teachers' collective belief in their ability to positively affect students (Hattie, 2018).

There are two types of beliefs that comprise the construct of efficacy. The first is personal teaching efficacy. This relates to your feeling of confidence about your teaching abilities. The second is general teaching efficacy, which "appears to reflect a general belief about the power of teaching to reach difficult children" (Hoy, 2000). Experts and researchers have found that these two constructs are independent, meaning you may have faith that teachers can reach students who struggle to learn, but you may lack confidence in your ability to work with some learners (Protheroe, 2008). Both constructs, however, can be impacted by mastery and vicarious experience. Mastery experience, the most powerful source of self-efficacy, develops through past successful accomplishments. Vicarious experience is attained through what teachers observe, hear, and read and what they learn from each other, which can be fostered through PLCs and instructional rounds. Teacher efficacy is strengthened when teachers observe effective instruction by their peers.

The research on collective teacher efficacy provides further reason to create a more diverse PLC that has various areas of expertise. One great activity to determine the strengths of your PLC is to start with a self-assessment to reflect on your own personal teaching efficacy. Yes, it will be scary and require vulnerability. Still, it is so important to recognize the power of bringing together different strengths and needs as you collectively design units that have the potential to improve outcomes for all learners. The process outlined next is one we often use when working with PLCs to help them "divide and conquer" aspects of curriculum design and recognize the incredible variability among the team. Additionally, it may highlight areas where all team members would benefit from support—it is incredibly important to advocate for professional learning opportunities in those spaces that can build your collective efficacy.

Whether you're a well-oiled PLC machine or meeting together for the first time, it's valuable to practice self-awareness and reflect on the variability of the team. At the beginning of this process, encourage all teachers to take a self-assessment using a rating tool scale (such as 1 to 4 from Strongly Agree to Strongly

Disagree). Table 3-2 includes sample questions that we use when we work with PLCs. You may use these, adapt them, or add to them depending on the focus areas of your school/district.

Table 3-2. Teacher Self-Assessment on Inclusive Practice

★ I feel prepared to engage all my students in learning by giving them choices and autonomy by incorporating their interests into the subject area/s I teach.

★ I feel prepared to design multiple and varied options so all learners can choose how they interact with content, learn new knowledge and skills, and share what they know.

★ I feel prepared to support all students in learning grade-level standards even if they do not speak English.

★ I feel prepared to support all students in learning grade-level standards even if they have significant support needs or are significantly behind their peers.

★ I feel prepared to support all students in learning grade-level standards even if they have significant behavior issues.

★ I feel prepared to support students who have significant needs for acceleration and enrichment.

★ I feel prepared to integrate restorative practices into academic instruction.

★ I feel prepared to integrate character education into academic instruction.

★ I feel prepared to integrate social-emotional learning into academic instruction.

★ I feel prepared to universally design instruction that supports students in succeeding on more standardized measures (state tests, AP exams, SAT, etc.).

There are multiple strategies for minimizing the threat of completing this self-assessment. For example, you can ask educators to note the areas where they have strong agreement so they identify areas where they feel they can lead without having to identify areas of weakness.

Another strategy is to ask everyone to choose the one statement that they most strongly agree with as well as the one that they most strongly disagree with. For example, a teacher may say that they feel most prepared to universally design instruction that supports students in succeeding on more standardized measures (state tests, AP exams, SAT, etc.) but feel the least prepared to support all students learning grade-level standards even if they do not speak English. This does not mean your colleague isn't prepared to support multilingual learners, but it's the area where they would benefit from the most support. If no one on your team felt that supporting multilingual learners was a strength, you would definitely need to invite the English language support teacher to join your meetings and/or have a book study on supporting multilingual learners!

If you do an activity like this in a Google Form, you can also reflect on the variability or the jaggedness of your team, as you can visualize that we all have strengths and areas where we would benefit from support.

Once your PLC completes a self-assessment, you can identify teachers whose sense of personal self-efficacy is strong in certain areas, and they can take the lead on focusing on that area as you unpack firm goals, design inclusive assessments, and co-plan universally designed units that meet the needs of all learners.

To build vicarious experience, you can also observe teachers who report strong feelings of efficacy in certain areas to learn from them and build your own personal efficacy. If you're not in the same school, you may video-record your practice to set up virtual instructional rounds.

It's important to emphasize that instructional rounds are not formal observations. Teachers are not assessed on anything, and there is no teacher rubric or grading system attached to the process. This is simply an opportunity for teachers to see other teachers in real classroom situations and then engage in the valuable opportunity to discuss what they saw with their peers while addressing problems of practice. While there are plenty of formatted ways to engage in instructional rounds, it is important that the norms for this process are collectively determined and that all participants are comfortable with the process (Novak & Woodlock, 2022). Table 3-3 adapts one of the considerations from the self-assessment process into a problem of practice with corresponding focus questions for instructional rounds. Note how focus questions can help teachers focus on instructional strategies that will help build collective efficacy.

Table 3-3. Common Problems of Practice and Focus Questions

Self-assessment prompts	Problem of practice	Focus questions for observation
I feel prepared to engage all my students in learning by giving them choices and autonomy by incorporating their interests into the subject area/s I teach.	Not all students have access to choices and autonomy in their learning environments.	★ How does the teacher provide firm goals and flexible means to learners? ★ Where do students have choices in how they learn? ★ Where do students have choices in the materials they use? ★ Where do students have choices in how they share their learning? ★ How does the teacher scaffold the choice-making process to support student autonomy? ★ How are students' interests incorporated into the design of the lesson?

As much as it's important to create a core PLC team, it's also valuable to invite special guests to support your planning process. Think of various stakeholders who can support your learners and be a part of your outer planning circle. Maybe they can join for a special PLC meeting to share their expertise and feedback on unit design and/or provide key insight about how to address students

who may not be learning at high levels. The following considerations may be helpful as you reflect:

- ⬭ How can you involve parents and students in your PLC,
  given that they bring different perspectives than those of
  educators?

- ⬭ Do you have a local bookstore or library that would love
  to get involved? Could they help you with choosing books
  or designing authentic assessments like writing to local
  authors?

Although it may seem odd to invite students to join the PLC, it
can be incredibly valuable to have them there in person or to bring
their voices to your PLC. Believe us. We tried it!

After we finished our first revised unit that incorporated UDL,
character education, and restorative practice, we started asking for
feedback from the students. It was positive and we felt like we were
moving in the right direction. However, one suggestion that we
received consistently from students was that our explicit vocabulary instruction felt like busywork and didn't improve reading
comprehension. They felt there were too many words to authenti-
cally learn. This was an aha moment for us and a great example of
a time when student feedback improved our design process.

If you can determine trends in student feedback, you can put
your heads together and begin to explore best practices in engagement and ongoing vocabulary instruction. Having student voice to
supplement academic artifacts when you reflect on the question
"How will we know if they learn it?" can be incredibly powerful
to drive choices in the future while celebrating and honoring student voice.

Creating Your PLC Vision

Your PLC is assembled, and you're ready to approach the work.
UDL is all about setting firm goals, so doing so for your work

together will be critical to maximizing your time. It might be helpful for your team to create a vision for your work. In the book *Universally Designed Leadership*, Novak and Rodriguez (2016) discuss the importance of a collective visioning process, as diverse perspectives in the planning process will strengthen the quality and effectiveness of the resulting curriculum plan. Here is a simple and clear plan for creating your curriculum vision:

1. Break into teams of two or three people and write a draft for the ultimate vision for your PLC work.

2. Coming back together as a group, small groups share their initial vision statements. Highlight critical components and work to merge them into a single vision statement. You may choose to type on a shared doc, project the draft on a screen, or use chart paper. One vision that guided our work was, "We will increase student engagement and access to grade-level standards by creating a responsive curriculum that incorporates high-interest texts, UDL, social-emotional learning, character education, and restorative practices. In our practice and in assessments, we will use innovative technologies to provide students with authentic opportunities to share their voice."

Before you plan your vision, it may be helpful to review your district strategy so you can proactively incorporate important frameworks into your curriculum design process. For example, many districts are focused on deeper learning, culturally responsive teaching and learning, and trauma-informed teaching. You may want to incorporate these critical frameworks into your vision so it doesn't feel like these things are in addition to your curriculum work. Rather, they are a core component of it.

As you read the previous sample vision statement, you may question the integration of innovative technologies. As we design our curriculum and instruction, we have to remember that COVID-19 and ChatGPT have changed the educational learning landscape. A good guide to follow as you consider how to use technology in your learning environment is the Triple E Framework developed by Professor Liz Kolb at the University of Michigan's School of Education (see Table 3-4). The Triple E Framework stands for "Engagement in learning goals, Enhancement of learning goals, and Extension of learning goals" (Kolb, 2017, p. 5).

Table 3-4. Triple E Framework, Adapted From Kolb (2020)

Engage learning	★ Does the technology allow the students to **focus on the task** of the assessment with less distraction? ★ Does the technology **motivate** students to start the learning process? ★ Does the technology cause a shift in the behavior of the students, where they move from passive to **active social learners (co-use or co-engagement)**?
Enhance learning	★ Does the technology tool aid students in developing or demonstrating a more **sophisticated understanding** of the content? ★ Does the technology **create scaffolds** to make it easier to understand concepts or ideas? ★ Does the technology create paths for students to demonstrate their understanding of the learning goals in a way that they **could not with traditional tools**?
Extend learning	★ Does the technology create opportunities for students to **learn outside** of the typical school days? ★ Does the technology create a bridge between school learning and **everyday life** experiences? ★ Does the technology allow students to **build skills** that they can use in their everyday lives?

Putting Your Vision Into Action

Keep in mind the Chinese proverb, "Be not afraid of growing slowly, be afraid only of standing still." Take that leap! You have a vision, but you don't have to accomplish it overnight. Instead, determine realistic lead measures that will move you forward. In *The Four Disciplines of Execution*, a book focused on improving strategic execution in corporate settings, McChesney, Covey, and Huling (2012) discuss the importance of lead measures or concrete action steps as you work toward your goals. You can help to guide goal-setting by being clear about your team's lead measures with statements like, "We will incorporate choices, aligned to firm goals, into assessments at least once a week," or "We will facilitate a restorative circle as a part of our core curriculum at least once in every unit." Determining realistic lead measures can help you target your work and make revisions to your curriculum over time. Remember that Rome wasn't built in a day (although—fun fact—Ryan said there was a mini-mall near his house erected in two days!). The following may be great places to begin your journey. These are all realistic goals for PLCs as long as you continue to reflect on the four core questions:

- Do you have a lesson plan you created years ago that you would like to revisit and redesign? How can you breathe new life into it? Will you make the lesson interactive? Can you incorporate UDL, social-emotional learning, character education, or restorative justice?

- Is there a lesson you have been thinking of making but haven't had inspiration for yet? This may be a great place for your team to start! You can reflect on the firm goal of the lesson, identify potential barriers, and use your collective expertise to begin to integrate options and choices as well as elements of social-emotional learning, character education, and/or restorative justice.

- If you want to start by making assessments more authentic and engaging, set a lead measure to add further options to supplement your current assessments. Always remember to ensure that all options are construct-relevant and lead to mastery of the same grade-level standards.

English teachers in PLCs who are proficient in UDL significantly enhance the effectiveness of their PLCs. As an example, incorporating SEL and restorative practices into design work can help teachers develop positive relationships with students and with each other, as they work to model positive behaviors and encourage growth and learning. Moreover, by understanding the social-emotional needs of students and creating a safe and supportive learning environment, teachers can leverage these practices to build trust and rapport with their colleagues in the PLC, which can improve communication, problem-solving, and decision-making. And goodness knows, even on well-functioning teams, conflicts will arise. When PLCs leverage restorative practices to address conflicts and repair harm, they model positive behaviors and help build a community of respect and trust. That's a PLC we all want to be a part of!

Committing to Continuous Improvement

The very nature of a PLC requires a commitment to continuous improvement. When you make changes in your instructional practice, it is critical that you determine the impact on all learners—which entails so much more than academic achievement using standardized measures. When you embrace the integration of these four frameworks into your ELA course, you'll need to continually plan, reflect, and improve, but you don't have to do this alone. In addition to your core PLC, working with students, families, and colleagues can help you to design a curriculum that values the four domains of literacy while also supporting students' self-awareness, voice, relationships, and overall well-being.

After you have incorporated your first lead measures, you're just beginning. Even after you've designed lessons and units, or even a whole curriculum, it's not fully baked, because PLCs are cyclical and always focus on the students you currently serve. A curriculum could work amazingly with students for one year and then different kids lead to different outcomes. A PLC's work is ongoing.

The bottom line: It's okay to miss the mark. It's okay to make mistakes. The very structure of a PLC allows for that as you continually ask, "What will we do if students don't learn?" This provides us with another chance, another opportunity, to learn from each other, to listen to students, and to grow. So know that as you lean into this journey, it's okay to fail. In fact, it's expected. But failure isn't permanent, especially when you have a team to keep you moving forward. This is how we all learn.

Reflection Questions

1. Why is collaboration so important when changing teaching practice? Think about times in your life when you experienced the power of collective efficacy. What was the experience like for you?

2. Reflect on your current PLC model. How do your discussions compare to the four core questions of PLCs through the lens of UDL?

3. How could you use the collective self-assessment process in this chapter to help identify and elevate relative strengths in your PLC?

4. How could instructional rounds support the collective efficacy of your PLC as you work to universally design your English language arts classrooms?

4

Unpacking Student Engagement

Be Kind, Rewind

The 1980s movie quotes scattered throughout this book are no mistake. It makes perfect sense when you realize that three out of five members of our team are Generation X. Thank goodness for that because we got to experience the 1986 film *Rad*. (Note: If you haven't watched this movie yet, make it a priority. You will thank us!) In one epic scene, the main character, Cru, rides in to prom on his BMX bike while a 1983 remix of "Send Me an Angel" plays. What preteen could resist this? But times have changed. The students we serve today never had to ride their bikes to a local Blockbuster to rent a VHS tape. They weren't reminded to "be kind, rewind," so the next renter didn't have to spend 10 minutes rewinding the tape back to the beginning. They don't have to wait. Everything they need is at their fingertips, and goodness gracious, it's hard to compete with that.

The term "digital natives" is familiar to most educators. Students that we serve today have never lived in a world without Wi-Fi, smartphones, or computers. Want to keep up with the most current hairstyles and learn to DIY ombre highlights? It's as easy as watching a TikTok video or Instagram reel. The saying "there's an app for that" is famous for a reason! Studies have shown that digital natives often learn better through active, kinesthetic learning (Bouronikos, 2021). Sitting behind a desk listening to the teacher's lecture doesn't work for most students anymore. (We argue it never really worked, but students were a little better at self-regulation.)

In another classic throwback, the 1986 film *Ferris Bueller's Day Off* includes scenes of a teacher calling "Bueller, Bueller, Bueller" over and over again during roll call, getting zero response from his class. The scene is funny until you realize that as a teacher, you know all too well what that feels like.

Engagement is so much more than interest, motivation, and participation. Engagement requires our learners to be purposeful and motivated, so they can challenge themselves, collaborate, self-regulate, and reflect. It requires learners to put in effort and commitment and continually strive to reach goals that are authentic and meaningful. Instead of thinking of engagement as something that is always observable or as a "fun meter," think about it as three elements—behavioral, emotional, and cognitive—which are sometimes hidden from the teacher (Fredricks, Blumenfeld & Paris, 2004). Each element can be defined as follows and is illustrated in Figure 4-1:

- **Behavioral engagement** consists of the observable indicators of cognitive and emotional engagement. Educators can observe students leaning forward, smiling, taking notes, and participating in class. These behaviors show interest and participation, but they may not reveal the true depth and breadth of learner engagement, motivation, and purpose.

- **Emotional engagement** describes the feelings students have about your learning environment, the curriculum and instruction, and learning in general. These feelings can range from confusion and anxiety to excitement and anticipation, and include apathy. When one is engaged in an activity that brings enjoyment or curiosity, one tends to invest more time and effort, which is why it's critical to provide meaningful options and choices to increase student interest, thereby potentially impacting behavioral engagement.

⊃ **Cognitive engagement** is about students learning at high levels. Generally, when students are cognitively engaged, they are committed to using the thinking skills described in Bloom's taxonomy, and they are willing to challenge themselves deeply and carry the cognitive load of learning. Because cognitive engagement can cause cognitive disso-nance, it's important that we continually ask students to self-reflect, take breaks, and self-regulate while they are learning.

A balance of the three elements of engagement allows students to become more expert in their learning while experiencing posi-tive emotions and outcomes.

Behavioral Elements   Emotional Engagement   Cognitive Engagement

Figure 4-1. The three elements of student engagement

We'll always think of teaching and learning as Pre-COVID (PC) and After-COVID (AC) because the considerations for the design and delivery of curriculum and instruction were forever changed when learning was forced out of schools and into homes, cars, and parking lots. This experience came with little warning, which forced us all into extremely interesting, challenging, and, at times, hilarious situations. While we all certainly found the COVID years arduous and demanding, we feel that they also gave educators the opportunity to reflect upon best practices in our educational environments. We were forced to think outside the box about how to minimize the very real barriers that students face.

Although face-to-face classrooms are back, we recognize that many student needs are still not being met, and student engagement is still a challenge. And did we mention ChatGPT and the disruption that chatbots will create? Don't even get us started!! While advanced tools like ChatGPT can provide students with access to vast amounts of information and can even help them complete tasks more efficiently, it's important to recognize that learning is a process that goes beyond simply acquiring information or completing tasks. Active engagement is critical to ensuring that students not only are able to master content and skills, but also develop the critical thinking, problem-solving, and collaboration skills that are essential for success in school and beyond.

When students are highly engaged in their learning, they're more likely to be motivated, curious, and invested in the learning process. They're more likely to take ownership of their learning and develop a deeper understanding of the material. Technology tools like ChatGPT can be most effective when used in conjunction with high levels of student engagement. The key is to use technology as a supplement to, not a replacement for, high-quality instruction and meaningful student engagement. Because goodness knows, if tools like ChatGPT supplant student critical thinking, creativity, and problem-solving, we will lose to the damn robots.

Why Maslow Before Bloom?

Most of us in the field of education are familiar with Abraham Maslow's hierarchy of needs, as it's at the core of our everyday work. The image of a tiered pyramid comes to mind for most of us, or possibly takes us back to a Psychology 101 college course. Maslow uses a pyramid to present his hierarchy of needs. The order is significant. The bottom of the pyramid indicates our basic needs and at the top are higher-level intangible needs. According to Maslow's theory, a person can only move on to addressing higher-level needs when their basic needs are adequately fulfilled. Maslow's theory of motivation includes five categories of human needs: Physiological, Safety, Love and Belonging, Esteem, and Self-Actualization (Figure 4-2).

Figure 4-2. Maslow's hierarchy of needs

In basic terms, you can't focus on learning with a rumble of hunger in your belly! If you don't have a roof over your head or adequate clothing for the weather, why would you care about reading an excerpt of *I Am Malala* in class? Spoiler alert: You don't. Engagement in learning is an esteem need that includes the desire to feel respected, valued, and competent. To engage our learners, we have to ensure that their more basic needs are being met—hence the importance of social-emotional learning and restorative practices, which help us create a learning environment that values safety, love, and belonging.

Ultimately, prior to delivering our universally designed ELA lesson, we need to ensure that the basic needs of our students are met. Have we checked in with our students? Did we greet them at the door to (hopefully) identify any outstanding areas of need? Maybe we notice that a student is wearing the same outfit four days in a row and it hasn't been laundered. Students' basic needs have to be met before they can engage in high levels of learning.

In 1956 Benjamin Bloom and colleagues published a framework for categorizing educational goals called the Taxonomy of Educational Objectives. Most of us know this framework as Bloom's taxonomy. When teachers refer to Bloom's taxonomy, we're really just talking about higher-level thinking and understanding. As Figure 4-3 shows, there are six major categories in the original 1956 publication: knowledge, comprehension, application, analysis, synthesis, and evaluation.

The years went by and another group of brilliant cognitive psychologists published a revision of the taxonomy in 2001. This group focused on transforming the original terms into "action words" on how we think and work with knowledge. The switch from nouns to verbs in labeling categories brought some life into the discussion of Bloom's original publication. Figure 4-4 shows the transformation of the six categories: remember, understand, apply, analyze, evaluate, and create. Note how all of these actions

Higher-order thinking skills

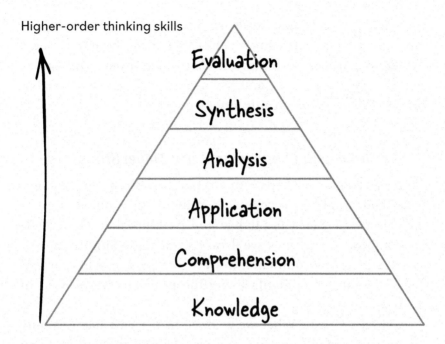

Lower-order thinking skills

Figure 4-3. Bloom's taxonomy

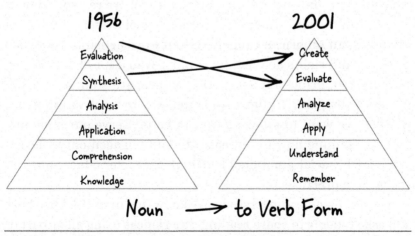

Figure 4-4. Bloom's 1956 taxonomy vs. the revision from Anderson and Krathwohl, 2001 (adapted from Wilson, 2001)

are learning and esteem needs, so if we want to increase behavioral, emotional, and cognitive engagement, we have to create a community where students can share their lived experiences, advocate for their needs, and feel safe enough to learn, collaborate, and share their learning among peers.

Increasing Engagement in a Novel Study

Now that you have a better understanding of how engagement is defined, you likely recognize that increased student engagement is more than compliance and participation—but goodness knows, sometimes we'll take even that! Simply, in our own learning environments, we recognize that it is harder and harder to engage students using the practices we've used in the past.

And let's face it: What we've done in the past has certainly not worked for all learners. It's also helpful to keep in mind that what works today might not work tomorrow. Education is ever-evolving, so we can't stick with the status quo because it is easy and safe and has worked in the past. We have a duty as educators to continue to learn and unlearn. We're reminded of a line from the viral video "I Sued the School System" by Prince EA (2021), an American rapper, spoken word artist, music video director, and rights activist. It's a must-watch for all educators. In the video, Prince EA asks, "Do you prepare students for the future or the past?" If there's a better way to teach reading and writing, we want to know so we can better serve our students. So let's examine how to increase student engagement by leveraging UDL, social-emotional learning, character education, and restorative practices.

Let's reimagine a novel study. We know that many ELA teachers still ask students to share reading experiences using all or part of a novel. First, we'll unpack a traditional novel-study lesson based on how many of us experienced ELA when we were students. The teacher would haul a box of books from the archives with numbers in black Sharpie along the binding. Everyone in the class would be assigned a book, hoping that their own had a crisp cover and all the pages. Each night, we were assigned a chapter to read, and we would return to class to take pop quizzes to ensure we'd completed the reading. Sometimes, the teacher would have us read in class, using strategies like popcorn reading, choral reading, or taking turns reading paragraphs in order. Generally, there were writing prompts aligned to the text and on-demand essays we had to write in blue exam books using blue or black ink. Sometimes we loved the books; sometimes we didn't. If we were lucky, there was a movie to watch at the end. Somehow, even though most of us have experienced this scenario, we fell in love with books and reading.

Dragging in a box of hard copies of classic novels likely doesn't excite all students, and when we assign reading outside of class, it's difficult to know if students read the text or used friends or technology to get relevant information. Without deep engagement, novel studies may feel like a hamster wheel of reading, answering questions, discussing, and repeating. So, let's redesign a more traditional novel study into one that is more universally designed. Let's first start with how to choose the right novel.

In this chapter, we'll use the book *I Am Malala* by Malala Yousafzai and Christina Lamb. Malala provides a mirror not only to Pakistani girls but many other girls as well, giving them an opportunity to see themselves in her book. Although Malala's story is extreme, her strength and story of survival is one that many students can relate to.

Text sets are collections of texts focused on specific topics or standards. Oftentimes, a "short profound text" is used as an anchor text—in this case, *I Am Malala*—and then paired with other short profound texts, multimedia, and/or visual texts. One great method for building a text set is the Quad Text Set Method (see Table 4-1), which pairs the anchor text with a visual text, a factual text to provide additional background information, and a more informal text, like social media posts or blogs.

Table 4-1. Quad Text Set

A visual text, consisting of still images or a video clip, requires little reading but contributes quickly to background knowledge in a way that not only *tells* but also *shows*.	**One or more accessibly written factual texts** can fill gaps in knowledge that the author of the target text assumes readers possess.
A young adult text or a more informal source such as a blog, which could be either fiction or an information source, piques interest by demonstrating how the target text is relevant.	**Central complex text** comes from the model lesson.

When teaching *I Am Malala,* we used the text set shown in Table 4-2 to help students build background knowledge using the Quad Text Set Method. Offering multiple means of representation helps to build background knowledge, increase comprehension, and increase engagement. Additionally, exposing students to a variety of texts encourages them to compare and contrast, identify biases, and think critically about the themes and issues presented in the novel.

Table 4-2. Text Set for *I Am Malala*

Visual texts	Accessible factual text: Students will explore children's books about Malala
★ Malala's TED Talk, "How One Girl Stood Up for Education and Changed the World" ★ Watch: Malala Yousafzai's Nobel Peace Prize acceptance speech	★ *Malala: My Story of Standing Up for Girls' Rights* by Malala Yousafzai ★ *Malala's Magic Pencil* by Malala Yousafzai
Informal source	**Complex text**
★ Malala is active on Instagram and Twitter. Students will review her social media profiles as informal text.	★ The novel *I Am Malala*

It may seem like a lot of work to create the text sets, but it doesn't have to be! There are numerous options to make this process more efficient and involve students at the same time. One option is to shift the responsibility of creating the text set to learners. *The Shift to Student-Led*, a book by Katie and Catlin Tucker (2022), advocates for teachers co-planning with learners. When discussing text sets, they note:

> As an educator, you may feel pressure to create the text sets yourself, but in a universally designed blended learning environment, there is an incredible opportunity to co-create text sets with students. First, introduce the text that will anchor the instruction and then encourage students to create teams that will supplement the text set. One group of students could look for visual images that connect to the standard or content under study, while another group explores relevant podcasts, TED talks, or digital media. You may be concerned that students will not find relevant and authentic texts. If that is the case, you can minimize that barrier by co-creating a rubric for selection or you can share reputable sites students can explore to find paired texts.

After students explore the text set, you can provide them with options and choices to share their learning like in Table 4-3.

Table 4-3. *I Am Malala* Options for Expression

Firm goal	Analyze various accounts of a subject told in different mediums (e.g., a person's life story in both print and multimedia), determining which details are emphasized in each account.
Assessment prompt	★ Use the resources in the text set, and any others you find through your own research, to explore the life of Malala Yousafzai. As you explore, look for the most relevant experiences in her incredible life. After you have explored the resources, choose one option from the choice chart to complete your assignment. ★ In addition to choosing one of the options below, prepare a short annotated bibliography that notes which details were emphasized in each source.
Assessment options	Create a presentation on the major life events in the life of Malala Yousafzai using textual evidence from at least three (3) sources as well as visual images.	Imagine you are Malala and are asked to speak to a group of high school students. Write out your speech highlighting the major events in your life using textual evidence from at least three (3) sources as well as visual images.	If you have a better idea for how you can share the major events in Malala's life that uses evidence from at least three (3) sources as well as visual images, propose it!

Integrating Social-Emotional Learning and Character Education

As we shared in the previous chapter, you can integrate a focus on both social-emotional learning and character education through CASEL's 3 Signature Practices. For example, consider the following prompt for a welcoming activity, which could be used to prepare for the unit on *I Am Malala* to ensure that students have an opportunity to practice self-awareness while connecting to important core values that Malala portrays in her life's work. Before introducing the text set, you could prompt students:

> Think back to a time when you faced a challenge that required you to show perseverance, courage, or empathy. How did you handle that situation? Did you persevere through it, show courage despite difficulties, or practice empathy toward others? Share your experience.

The value of community circles is evident when we discuss the essential questions or focus on a character trait in a novel. We already have a clear understanding of agreements and trust, should any triggers arise as students begin to connect to the characters in the novel. Let's share an example from an ACE lesson design in action with *I Am Malala*. We revisit the essential question throughout the entire novel. Our essential question for *I Am Malala* is "How can one person's dedication lead to change?" The character trait we base daily discussions on for this novel is dedication. Students are encouraged and challenged to find relatability between themselves and the characters they are exploring. As a result, students begin to develop a vested interest in the journey and experiences of the character—in this novel, the character of Malala.

Abdul was an outgoing, vocal teenager with natural leadership qualities. He was headstrong and independent, but also a bit closed to the world. Abdul seemed to like the book *I Am Malala* even though he never outwardly gave his opinion, but he also seemed to be indifferent to the connectivity of the book and its content. During one welcoming activity, students were prompted, "Who is a person or group of people in your life who make you feel empowered?" At the end of the week, we collected the students' responses as we often did and noticed Abdul's response to this particular entry was exceptionally long. He shared that his own family had fled Syria's unrest and that his father had risked his life so that his family could be safe. Abdul also mentioned that he felt empowered to help others based upon his father's example, much like Malala. One never knows what or when something will resonate with a student, but when it happens, it has a profound and lasting effect.

Abdul used a more traditional means of responding to the prompt through writing. Keep in mind that in all of the unique settings where we teach, it is valuable to provide options and choices for how students respond.

Building Engagement Through Restorative Practices

As the late Rita F. Pierson said in her inspiring TED Talk, "Every Kid Needs a Champion," kids don't learn from people they don't like (Pierson, 2013). Successful teachers are champions of building relationships with students in support of classroom management, safety, and academic instruction. When students know they are a part of the process and that they have been heard, we can bridge the gap between presence and engagement. As we mentioned previously, the power of forming relationships and conversations in the safe restorative circle is that it gives students the opportunity to be heard and valued so we can help them become more self-aware and share their interests and passions. This relates to the *psychology of affect*.

The psychology of affect "asserts that human relationships are best and healthiest when there is free expression of affect—or emotion—minimizing the negative, maximizing the positive, but allowing for free expression" (Costello, Wachtel, & Wachtel, 2010, p. 41). This free and mutual expression of ideas, emotions, and feelings is a prominent argument for integrating restorative practices into our daily instruction. Not only do circles provide a cultural community and a safe place where the whole class develops a voice, but once the circles are established, they're a great way to discuss themes in a text deeply while connecting to students' lives and the challenges they face.

There are a few considerations that may be helpful as you think about preparing to facilitate circle practice. First, be sure to have a *talking piece*—an item that will be passed around the circle as each participant speaks. Only the person holding the talking piece can speak. Arrange chairs in a circle, including a chair for yourself as a facilitator. If your chairs are attached to desks, turn the desks around to create a circle or even a square if necessary. The goal is to intentionally design the room for equity of voice. The reality is that some of us work in extremely unique conditions and will need to get creative. We get it.

 Restorative circles are a perfect match for ELA classes since we have speaking and listening standards to address. This allows us to use restorative circles as forms of assessment where students can demonstrate mastery as they engage in meaningful dialogue, active listening, and collaborative problem-solving. Restorative circles are a powerful tool for achieving these standards, creating a safe and supportive environment where students can share their thoughts and feelings, listen actively to others, and work together to address common challenges.

It's important to have shared *agreements* for your restorative circles. Agreements are the expectations or rules created by the class for the discussion time. You could connect the agreements to your core values, which allows you to integrate character education into the circle process. To create agreements, it may be helpful to reflect on the following suggestions (Boyes-Watson & Pranis, 2020). (Note that a *round* is a full circuit of the talking piece around the circle. The facilitator poses a question and, as a participant, usually answers first. The facilitator then passes the talking piece to the left or right. It's always okay for a participant to pass.)

1. Have each participant take an index card and write a quality or value—such as honesty, respect, or sharing—that they express when they are at their best. This is a great connection to social-emotional learning and character education.

2. The facilitator will go first and share what they wrote on their index card and place it in the center of the circle.

3. In a round, every student is invited to participate. Some may choose to pass. Let those who passed know that you will revisit after everyone has gone to see if they would like to contribute at that time.

4. In a round, ask, "What agreements do you need from yourself or others in order to be at your best here in this classroom?" Write down what students are saying on chart paper, poster paper, or in a shared digital document. Combine and capture as much as possible.

5. In a round, ask students if they can agree to try to do what you've written. Are there some agreements that participants aren't willing to try to keep? If you feel that anything should be added, this is the time to bring it to the group. You're included in the community and have a voice as well.

6. Explain that agreements or guidelines aren't the same as rules; they're reminders of the kind of behaviors we want from others and ourselves. They are not imposed by others on the group but are decided on together.

7. In a round, ask, "Which one of these agreements would be easiest for you to honor? Which one would be the most difficult or challenging for you?"

8. At the end, in a round, ask students to share how they felt about the circle practice and the creation of norms.

Once you've reviewed the agreements and made connections to core values, you've established the norms that will help to facilitate future circles. Now let's dive into what circle practice could look like for *I Am Malala.* We offer the following questions, which integrate self-awareness and reflection, character education, and the value of building relationships in a restorative circle. Using these questions in circle practice can help to build behavioral, emotional, and cognitive engagement with the text as students make text-to-self connections.

- What did you admire about Malala and her activism for girls' education?

- How does Malala's story relate to the experiences and struggles of girls and women around the world?

- How can we apply the lessons from Malala's story to our own lives and communities?

- How can we be allies to those who are fighting for their rights, just like Malala did?

Note how these questions can be used to facilitate a circle, but the circle can also act as a prewriting opportunity for students as they brainstorm and share their own experiences.

Reflection Questions

1. UDL engagement requires behavioral, emotional, and cognitive engagement so all learners are motivated and purposeful. What are some of the barriers to student engagement in your learning environment? How can UDL, SEL, character education, and restorative practice create a foundation for more authentic engagement?

2. How can you empower students to help pair texts to create more culturally responsive text sets that increase student engagement?

3. A key component of engagement is interpersonal relationships in the classroom. Social-emotional learning and restorative practices allow us to foster relationships honoring student voice. What are some other ways to help students build relationships with one another in your learning environment?

5

Fostering a Love of Reading

A Knife in the Heart

Ryan Hinkle

I have always been an avid reader. Since I was very young, I always had a book in my hand and considered reading more than just a hobby . . . it was an obsession. I can still remember the first book that I read on my own: *Ramona and Her Father* by Beverly Cleary. I recall the autonomy, pride, and achievement after I finished that book and couldn't wait to start another. So where did the obsession start? Clearly, I was not born with the love of reading. And I don't recall being overly excited about the *See Spot Run* books in kindergarten. Luckily, I had parents who read to me often as a child. I still reminisce about the days when my parents would conclude the day with an elaborate picture book. Before tackling my first book, I got in the habit of stacking various comic books, California Angels programs, brochures, and picture books that I would peruse nightly before falling asleep. It's a ritual I still practice. I cannot sleep soundly until I dive into some Neil Gaiman, Stephen King, or Mark Twain. So, I assumed my love for reading was based on my parents' influence. I would simply employ the same methods with my kids and get a similar result. Spoiler alert: It did not work out that way.

From the time my oldest son, Lukas, was very little, my wife and I read to him before bed. We had a plethora of books to choose from, as we obtained a number of hand-me-downs from family members with older children, yet Lukas would typically pick the same 10 books. His all-time favorites were *Tikki Tikki Tembo* by Arlene Mosel, *So Say the Little Monkeys* by Nancy Van Laan, and *The Monster at the End of This Book* by Jon Stone. We would attempt to introduce him to other titles, but he always went back to his favorites. I am quite certain that I can still recite *Tikki Tikki Tembo* verbatim. I know he can.

I was mimicking exactly what my parents had done with me when I was my son's age, and I couldn't wait until he was old enough to read his first novel and experience the same adoration I had years before. The day finally arrived. He came home from school with his first novel—not a short, 20-page reading assignment but an actual multichapter, 100-plus-page novel: *The Hatchet* by Gary Paulsen. Part of it was read aloud in class, but his teacher had assigned a significant amount of the book to be read independently. Once Lukas started, I couldn't wait for him to run into our room and discuss it with vigor and excitement. A few hours passed and still nothing. Perhaps he was so into his book that he was reading beyond the assigned pages. More time passed, and still nothing. I went into his room, expecting an enthusiastic account, and was met instead with a very frustrated young boy. When I asked him about the issue, his response was like a knife in my heart: "Dad, I hate reading."

How could this happen? I did everything right! I read to him nightly and developed an environment where he was encouraged to read for pleasure. Obviously, there was more to this "love for reading" conundrum than I had originally thought.

Why Kids Don't Read Like They Used To

In the 1970s, teens read significantly more than they do today. In the 1980s, 60 percent of high school students indicated that they read some type of print material on a daily basis. In 2016, that number was only 16 percent (Twenge, Martin, & Spitzberg, 2019). This trend is troubling indeed, as we know the benefits and advantages for those who read regularly.

Multiple studies have found that print exposure is important for the development of vocabulary, reading comprehension, fluency, and improved technical reading and spelling skills. While students in primary grades tend to read for pleasure at a much higher rate than their adolescent counterparts, it is much less prevalent than it was in the past. Furthermore, in the past, primary-grade students who were avid readers continued to read into their adolescence and adulthood. Sadly, we no longer see this trend. Why are we seeing such a drastic change in print exposure in students, especially at the middle and high school level?

The digital age has been an exciting and revolutionary sea change in education. We have a plethora of educational web tools that can be used in our curriculum in a productive and engaging way. But the digital age has some downsides as well, which are having a devastating effect on literacy.

Compared to when we were young (okay, we are definitely dating ourselves), the distractions and instant gratifications available to students are staggering. We're going to sound like our grandparents, but when we were young, there wasn't a lot to do when you got home from school except complete your homework and play outside with your friends. You may have found a single channel with afternoon cartoons, and if you were lucky, you could catch an episode of *Speed Buggy*, but that only lasted 30 minutes.

Today, most students have access to 300+ channels and streaming services operating 24 hours a day. That was unheard of when we were kids. We had 13 channels that shut off around midnight with a test pattern. (We can just see everyone born after 1982 googling "test pattern.") Sadly, television is the least of the distractions constantly available to students, which include video games, computer games, TikTok, YouTube, and the biggest culprit of them all: the smartphone.

Research has shown that adolescents are actually developing addiction-like behaviors associated with their smartphones (Wacks & Weinstein, 2021). It has been well documented that text messages actually activate the same part of the brain as opiates (Small, 2009). While this is alarming, let's be realistic: The smartphone isn't going away. In fact, it's only going to be a bigger distractor that will limit a student's overall attention level. It seems fairly evident that reading is naturally going to take a back seat to a handheld device that mimics a narcotic and is currently the only way many students communicate.

The digital generation's brains have changed because they've grown up with information at their fingertips. As educators, we are facilitators of learning rather than the givers of information. Gary Small, a psychiatry professor and director of the University of California, Los Angeles, Longevity Center at the Semel Institute for Neuroscience and Human Behavior, stated in an *Atlantic* article that "during adolescence, each person's brain weeds out the pathways that it uses less often in a process called neural pruning. In other words, if you spent your youth in front of screens, it would make sense that your adult brain would be hard-wired to process information at a frenzied pace" (Ossola, 2014).

 It's never been more important for students to have opportunities to read printed text, if it can be made accessible, in English language arts. Numerous studies have argued that reading printed text helps to offset some of the negative impacts of frequent screen use and digital reading on attention and reading stamina. An *EdWeek* article reported on a recent study that found "students at all ages tend to favor reading in print more than online and report growing tired more quickly when reading digitally, which some studies have credited to increased eyestrain from reading smaller or backlit text. But the biggest difference between digital and print reading seems to come from digital interactivity. Including hyperlinks, videos, and other interactive elements encourages students to jump around on the story and among texts on different pages, rather than reading linearly" (Sparks, 2019).

The findings of the study have several implications for ELA classrooms. First, although technology can help make texts more accessible and flexible, we have to be mindful of digital elements such as hyperlinks, videos, and other interactive elements, which can also lead to distraction and disengagement. As we design lessons through the lens of UDL, it will also be important to teach students how to navigate digital texts effectively, including strategies for managing distractions, maintaining focus, and engaging with the material in a meaningful way (see the connection to social-emotional learning there!). As English teachers, we can play an essential role in helping students develop these skills, which will be increasingly critical in our digital age.

What is the most effective environment for reading? We would likely all agree that a quiet setting with few to no distractions is ideal, even though our students may argue otherwise. Katie often listens to Audible while she runs but loves being beachside or poolside with a paperback book and a piña colada. Ryan personally prefers a quiet beach in Brazil. Jina enjoys reading at a local coffee shop with noise-cancelling earbuds in while she escapes into her current book. A little boring, but who are we to judge? (We love you, Jina!) If Anne had her wish, she'd be nestled snugly next to a Grindylow at the study hall in Hogwarts Castle. Brianne simply wants any environment where she's not constantly hounded by her husband and three kids. Sadly, Brianne does not read much.

When we read or even listen to books, we either turn off our phones or turn off the notifications to minimize distractions. It's hard to get lost in a book if you can't find your way there. Students actually read all day: blogs, memes, tweets, texts, and the like. However, this isn't considered print exposure; rather, it's transitory text that is often grammatically subpar and written in a colloquial, casual manner. Students need to be exposed to long-form texts in order to develop complex ideas and critical thinking skills. With all of that against us as educators, how do we get kids to start reading again?

Choosing the Right Novel

We argue that all units should be grounded in high-quality texts that help students fall in love with their literacy lives. When we universally design instruction, we can honor students by allowing them to choose their own texts. We, of course, however, want them to choose high-quality texts that matter. A high-quality text is one that is appropriately complex and includes four core aspects of text quality: conventions, organization, content, and reader interest (Louis, 2013). Consider sharing the criteria in Table 5-1 with groups of students to help them choose meaningful texts that matter.

Table 5-1. Criteria for High-Quality Texts (Adapted From Louis, 2013)

Trait	Criteria
Conventions	★ Errors are so few and minor that a reader could skip right over them unless searching for them. ★ The text appears clear, edited, and polished.
Organization	★ The entire piece has a strong sense of direction and balance. ★ An inviting lead pulls the reader in, while a satisfying conclusion provides a sense of closure. ★ Transitions are smooth, helpful, and natural. ★ Pacing is effective. The writer knows when to linger and when to move on.

Table 5-1 Continued. Criteria for High-Quality Texts (Adapted From Louis, 2013)

Trait	Criteria
Content	★ The writer's knowledge, experience, insight, and/or perspective lend the piece authenticity.
Reader interest	★ The writer's passion for the subject drives the writing, making the text lively and engaging. ★ The writing bears the imprint of the writer. ★ Word choice is original—even memorable—but not overdone. ★ Sentences are well structured and invite expressive oral reading.

Not every student will love the same book, even when that book meets the criteria for a high-quality text, but we can anchor our units in a text that students can pair with the texts that speak to their hearts. We need our students to experience, for at least a moment, what we experienced back when we fell in love with books.

Our team shares a common feeling of being predisposed or even pressured to introduce classic novels to our students. But if they're not interested, what's the point? Brianne mentioned that she can't remember a single student in 18 years who could identify with Nick Carraway's opulent lifestyle from *The Great Gatsby*. We argue that introducing high-interest and relevant novels into the curriculum has a profound effect on student learning and motivation. When we teach a child to swim, we certainly don't throw them into the deep end and hope for the best. We start small and build experiences where they develop confidence and autonomy. Yet we don't follow the same pattern with reading. We *do* throw students into the deep end and hope for the best. We think that we have a better method. Once you've articulated the firm goals, it's beneficial to select a complex grade-level text as an anchor text. If you have the flexibility to choose an anchor text, consider elevating and celebrating the voices of authors in identity groups who have been historically marginalized or minoritized. An article from *Harvard Ed* magazine, "Hooked on Classics" (Anderson, 2019), offers the following guidance:

> *The canon has long been revered in public education as representing the "depth and breadth of our national common experience" . . . the books that many believe all high school students should be studying. The problem is that what was once defined as "common"—middle class, white, cisgender people—is no longer the reality in our country. Unfortunately . . . "making a case for new literature by different authors of color, authors who are not cisgendered, or even just female authors" is a challenge.*

Again, it is important to note that we're not opposed to reading classic novels, especially excerpts of those novels, as long as they are accessible, paired with culturally responsive texts in multiple formats, and connected to texts that students can choose. The books considered to be classics are defined as such because they contain thought-provoking socio-ethical situations, allusions, symbolism, and rich text, and they're often challenging. This is indeed a valuable criterion, but we can reach these firm goals with much more flexible means. However, some classic novels can be problematic in the classroom, as their themes or messages can be troubling toward women, people of color, and those with mental or physical disabilities.

When students become interested in what is being read, their curiosity develops into motivation to read more. Instructional approaches or materials that are motivating, as well as teachers who show interest and enjoyment in the subject or activity, can sometimes lead to the development of long-term interest.

Our message collectively is this: It's okay to change. *I wanted to teach the way that I had been taught because it worked for me. Teaching methods are timeless, correct?* Obviously not, or we wouldn't take part in professional development seminars every year. It's okay to change! If what you are doing is not working for your students, it's time to try something different. As discussed earlier, students are different today than they were in your day, and they always will be. We need to find novels and extended texts that are meaningful to their lives and interests in order to bolster an emotional connection to that text.

Researchers have found that interest level has a profound effect on what students read, as well as the complexity of the text, the selection, and student comprehension (Springer, Harris, & Dole, 2017). This is supported as well by Schwanenflugel and Flanagan (2017), who found that "when readers have a good bit of prior knowledge on a topic, even difficult texts can be easier to read and understand because they can draw on their own knowledge to fill in any gaps in their comprehension."

Emotional connection, relevance, and engagement are closely interconnected when it comes to reading. When a reader feels emotionally connected to a text, they relate to the characters, the setting, or the events in the text. This emotional connection can make the text feel more relevant, which in turn can increase their engagement with the text. When a reader is engaged with a text, they are more likely to read it carefully and comprehend it fully because they are interested in it, pay attention to it, and remember it. This, in turn, can lead to improved reading skills and greater enjoyment of reading.

For one unit, we asked our students to help us choose a book, and after much discussion, we chose *Unwind* by Neal Shusterman, a novel that depicts a dystopian society that challenges the ethics and morals of parents and adolescents alike. We went all in and designed the lesson by incorporating UDL, restorative practices, and character education to reach all students. Would the design truly allow us to eliminate barriers? Two situations answered this question unequivocally.

First, a young man, 16, who had never actually, self-reportedly, finished a novel, not only finished *Unwind* ahead of the teaching schedule but went on his own and got a library card so he could check out the sequels. Second, a young cadet in a military program, who was scheduled to go home for the weekend, attempted to steal the novel because he couldn't wait to finish the book. Both students reported being nonreaders prior to finding a novel that not only could they relate to but whose main character they could see themselves in.

So, our advice is this: Keep your preferences at the door. We often hear from frustrated ELA teachers who can't believe that their students did not enjoy one of their favorite books. If you've had this experience, we feel your pain. Not surprisingly, novels that changed you years ago may not have the same effect on the students you serve. And we're speaking from experience. We realize that this can be tough. We are the college-educated adults in the room, right? So, how do we find the book that students want to read? Consider the following tips:

- Ask your students. After all, they are your target audience. Do they have a current book they can't put down? Do your students have an author they absolutely love? You can build this into an optimistic opener or a circle activity.

- Having to stay within the parameters of approved books is challenging but not impossible. Create a survey with three to five book options for students to rate and choose. This will allow for student voice but stay on point with expectations.

- Refer to the Young Adult Library Services Association (YALSA) Book and Media Awards to learn about different award-winning books for young adult readers. You might even discover a new favorite book for yourself.

- To find award-winning children's and young adult books that portray Latin America, the Caribbean, or Latinx in the

United States, check out the Consortium of Latin American Studies Programs (CLASP).

● Refer to the Association for Library Service to Children (ALSC) to see the latest books that have won the Caldecott Medal, Newbery Medal, Odyssey Award, and more.

● Connect with a local library or bookstore to see what their top sellers are for young adults. Would it be possible to partner with them to help you get books for your students?

When students have a strong interest in what they read, they can frequently transcend their reading level (Worthy, 1996). Yes, it's important that students access grade-level text, but a Lexile number shouldn't be the only deciding factor when we select texts for our learners. A *Lexile number* is simply a readability formula that assigns a reading level to texts based on word frequency and sentence length. Lexile level does have value in education when utilized in tandem with student interest and age-appropriate content, but as a standalone criterion, it can severely limit student choices, engagement, and comprehension of selected text. What's most important is that the student is interested and engaged in reading complex texts. Only then can we begin to design the types of learning experiences that allow all students to work toward grade-level standards in ways that are both challenging and supportive.

UDLing the Chosen Text

First, we recognize the barriers to handing out a hard copy of a novel, as printed text can create significant barriers for some learners. UDL reminds us to consider the barriers and how we can address them by providing additional options using the UDL principles. Table 5-2 highlights potential options and choices to make rigorous and relevant texts more accessible to learners.

Table 5-2. Approaches to Eliminate Barriers to Traditional Printed Text

Barriers	UDL guideline	How to eliminate
Text is inaccessible, so some students may not be able to decode or comprehend text at that level.	Provide multiple means of perception.	Offering students an audiobook, rich visuals, or opportunities to collaborate will support comprehension. Note: A low-tech option is to provide the option for students to join a small group where someone reads aloud.
Some students may be English learners.	Provide options for language and symbols.	Offering students an ebook as well as translation software can support language development as well as an audiobook, rich visuals, and opportunities to collaborate with sentence stems.
Some students may have visual impairments that make small font inaccessible.	Provide multiple means of perception.	Offering students an ebook where they can enlarge text or an audiobook can support decoding and comprehension.

Empowering Our Students to Create Their Own Reading Nooks

How did we discover our favorite places to read and escape into a good book? Is this a learned behavior, or did we naturally build a passion for reading and discover our favorite spots? This process can be learned, and a love of reading can come from seeing and experiencing the passion in others. Jina can remember a political science professor's passion for reading about and discussing the events of the Vietnam War. His passion and ability to engage students in the topic made Jina want more! Ryan remembers his eccentric 10th-grade English teacher who saw his love of Stephen King and opened up his world to Edgar Allan Poe, H. P. Lovecraft, and Mary Shelley. Both found quiet nooks in the library to escape with more books.

Providing creative and diverse in-class opportunities that model ways to focus and enjoy the love of reading is pretty powerful. Our team agrees that, much like our universally designed lessons, there is not just one correct answer. We brainstormed a few suggestions that we want to share:

- Set up a corner of the classroom with cozy seating for students to explore on breaks or free time.

- Set up a "Starbucks Time" slide to post when it is reading time, promoting a "coffee shop" sense of freedom. Allow students to work quietly and independently and to listen to music that motivates them on their earbuds, and remind them about social cues so they know when not to collaborate or interrupt peers.

- Involve students in the discussion. Have them come up with places on campus or ideas for creating a reading space in the classroom.

- Facilitate a circle and ask students to contribute their ideal distraction-free space to optimize voice and choice.

By providing a comfortable and inviting space that encourages students to explore books that represent their lived experiences, teachers can foster an environment that builds engagement and passion for reading. Allowing students to choose the texts that interest them and encouraging them to create their own reading nooks can help ensure that they are engaged and motivated to read.

In our community day schools, attendance and engagement are always a challenge. Imagine taking all of the students who either were expelled or unsuccessful in a traditional school setting and placing them all in one class. This is chaos! However, when we get it right, we really get it right! One dynamic example of the power of text choice and students designing their own reading environments is a student-requested book club prompted after they read Neal Shusterman's novel *Unwind*. The students solicited teachers to help organize an *afterschool* book club so they could read the sequel, *UnWholly*. Wait—what? Imagine at-promise students asking to stay after school to read! Yup, and believe it or not, not only did it work, but the number of participants grew!

The teachers reached out to Ryan, who was the teacher on special assignment (TOSA) at the time. A student, Manuel, was rushing through the Neal Shusterman novels, and he quickly, eagerly, and desperately wanted the next book in the *Unwind* series. This prompted Ryan to start a conversation with Manuel about a great resource where he can check out books and use them for free—a library! Manuel had never been to a public library; he'd only visited his elementary school library as a young child. Manuel was blissfully unaware of this land of free books. Ryan provided Manuel with all the information on how and where to get his library card. Ryan challenged him to go get a library card and check out the third book in the series, with a promise that if he followed through, Ryan would purchase the rest of the series for him to keep. Manuel is now the proud owner of all nine books in the *Unwind* series.

Wellness rooms are quickly becoming a norm at most of our school campuses. These rooms are designed by students and a "wellness team" comprising staff that support social and emotional health. The rooms often have dim lighting, comfortable seats (couches, bean bags, pillows, etc.), calming aromatherapy, and relaxing instrumental music. Students are encouraged to use this room to "unwind" (see what we did there! ha!) and as a nonjudgmental, calm space to relax or lose themselves in a fictional world that only a reader visits. We've found that the spaces are used frequently for reading, and student feedback is always used for improvement.

Revisiting Lukas

Ryan Hinkle

Let's return to the horrifying day when my son, Lukas, confessed he hated reading. Instead of exploring books that appealed to his background and interests, I continued to push books on him that he found boring and uninspiring. I was under the impression that the more he read, the more he would enjoy it. This was my mistake. Lukas has always been into computers and is in a tech program at our local high school. When he was in seventh grade, I gave him Ernest Cline's *Ready Player One* after I finished the book, as I thought it would be perfect for him. Lukas read the entire book in one day. Lukas's reaction was much like my reverence for my first novel. It changed his mind about reading and opened a veritable Pandora's box where we lost my son to his room for days at a time when he was glued to a book. This obsession has not abated for Lukas, and beyond the obvious benefits associated with reading, it also keeps him from Snapgramming and Instatoking with his friends at all hours of the day. On top of this, Lukas has created a new network of friends based solely on their love of reading.

Maybe he's following in my footsteps, after all. My oldest and best friend, Jason Lasher, is also an avid reader, and we've been trading good books back and forth for almost 40 years. I told Lukas how much we both loved reading and about how Jason and I used to rail about the novels and selected texts that we were forced to read in high school. When my son gets older, I will tell him about some of our wilder adventures, but for now, I'll stick with the benefits of reading.

Reflection Questions

1. What are the potential consequences of digital age technology on students' literacy, and how have you addressed them in your practice?

2. In this chapter, we discuss strategies to work with students to choose novels that represent their lived experiences. How can you use these strategies to choose a novel, or an excerpt of a novel, with your students?

3. Some students face barriers that prevent them from accessing grade-level text. How can UDL help identify and eliminate barriers so students can share reading experiences with complex texts?

4. What are some concrete ways, like working with students to build reading nooks, to create an environment that fosters their engagement and passion for reading?

6

Enhancing Vocabulary Instruction

Will Work for Free Subs

Brianne/Jina

Jesse was 17 when he entered the alternative education classroom. He had been kicked out of every school he had attended for most of his educational career, but he assured his teacher this time was different. This time he was getting his life together because he was almost 18 and going to be an "adult." Jesse's collared shirts and Dickies pants were always clean and freshly pressed with the perfect creases, just as the generations before him had worn them. He always walked in with a smile on his face that told you this kid owned the world, or at least his world. Jesse's calm, reassuring, and confident tone made him easy to listen to. He was a product of parents, grandparents, and extended family that had taught and instilled in him the importance of respecting and protecting your neighborhood at all costs. But they also instilled in him that education was of utmost importance and the "family business" should not interfere, unless completely necessary. Jesse assured us, with his confident and smooth demeanor, that he had changed. Jesse mentioned he was even actively looking for a job as a means to becoming a responsible adult. However, he'd applied to many places and either wouldn't get past the initial application screening or never made it past the interview. Jesse got discouraged and asked for help.

He brought in the applications for us to review, and we did a mock interview that included many common interview questions. Upon looking at Jesse's application for a sub shop, we noticed one prompt was "Explain why you want to work at this shop."

Jesse's response was, "This place is dope and homeboy says you get free subs." If we're being honest, we've cleaned up the language a bit for our audience. We read his answer aloud to him and asked if he thought this was the answer the manager was hoping for. Jesse looked bewildered, not sure if he was offended or confused, but definitely not rethinking his answer like we had hoped.

Jesse responded, "That's why I want to work at that place, it's got dope sandwiches and you get free stuff!" Again, we've cleaned up the language for our readers. You're welcome. It was clear that we had found the glitch. Jesse's vernacular was acceptable with his family and peers; however, he lacked the academic and workplace vocabulary needed to be employable! Fortunately, we had some tools to help him think about the task, purpose, and audience to communicate more effectively. We told him that certainly, he could tell his friends about the free subs (that *is* a sweet perk), but there may be a better way to sell himself to an employer. As you all know, it's critical that we ask students to reflect on task, purpose, and audience before they plan their communication.

As teachers of English, we must take into account that several factors contribute to effective communication, such as exposure to social and academic language, culture, and interpretation of verbal and nonverbal communication. A side eye or scrunch of the nose can be just as clear as a yell across the room and, used in partnership with spoken word, can create deeper meaning.

In today's climate, we have to also take into consideration social media, YouTube, GIFs, and memes.

Language helps us navigate our daily interactions as well as our academic life. The ability to decipher the correct tone or choose the appropriate words is critical for success in work and life. We must be careful not to police student language but rather to help students choose the best words for the task. To shed light on this point, we want to share a story from Jina's time as a reading intervention teacher. Most of us can relate to the feeling of our heart skipping a beat with nervousness when the principal walks in unannounced at lunch. Either they need a "volunteer," or you have intentionally or unintentionally done something that clearly elicits a discussion with the boss. To Jina's surprise, Dr. Miller came in and asked an unusual question. "Mrs. Poirier, did you happen to do a lesson on the word 'vernacular' today?" Jina replied with hesitation and a long, drawn-out "Yeeeeeeeessss?"

Dr. Miller shared that she walked into the lunch area and overheard one of our more vivacious and vocal students, Scott, tell another student to "watch their vernacular." As lunch continued, Dr. Miller heard yet another little cherub tell a student to "watch their vernacular." When she asked the students what vernacular meant, they nailed it! The students, confused and assuming they were in some type of trouble, proceeded to tell Dr. Miller to ask Mrs. Poirier about it, hence the visit. Exhale! Phew, this was actually a positive visit from the boss!

The lesson on the term *vernacular* came out of addressing an ongoing issue of language that wasn't exactly aligned with task, purpose, and audience. The cussing had taken on a life of its own. There are times when students cuss during class when they're passionate about telling a story or excited that they got the response right. Vanessa would shout out to her friend, "F*** yeah!" when she achieved a desired grade. Similarly, Lucas would often—or, well, actually almost always—use the f-word as every part of speech while expressing his knowledge of a subject or simply conversing with a classmate or teacher. In fairness, Lucas always used the word grammatically correctly. A simple smile and a reminder that we're in school works well in these scenarios—as does not bringing it up at all! After all, why would we want to diminish a student's excitement about something they're learning? bell hooks (2014) reminds educators to value all student language: "I know that it is not the English language that hurts me, but what the oppressors do with it, how they shape it to become a territory that limits and defines, how they make it a weapon that can shame, humiliate, colonize." Gloria Anzaldúa (1987) reminds us of this pain in *Borderlands/La Frontera* when she asserts, "So, if you want to really hurt me, talk badly about my language" (p. 168).

Jina didn't want to shame students for their language, but the cussing was exploding like a confetti cannon. It was time for some reflection and an impromptu vocabulary discussion.

Taking time to discuss the word *vernacular* and the value of using language spoken by a group of people who share a geographic region, cultural background, or "mother tongue," as well as knowing our audience and atmosphere, is of utmost importance! Although it seemed that the vernacular of the students included a lot of derogatory terms, it was important to honor the dialect that students used in their communities.

Jina explained that there would be no consequence for using inappropriate language in class "vernacular," but challenged the students to think about their audience and atmosphere before they chose their words. Interestingly, students chose to *not* use some of the words! It was clear that it was way more exciting to cuss when you're not supposed to. It was a bit flattering that they wanted to "watch their vernacular" in front of Jina.

The purpose of these stories is to highlight the value of students having an awareness of the vernacular used with their family and peers as well as the ability to code switch into professionally and academically appropriate language when the situation warrants. We want students to learn how to express themselves in ways that are culturally responsive, authentic, and unique, but they need to understand that there is power in words and there are certain things you probably shouldn't say in front of your grandma or in a job interview—much like Jesse, who quickly learned that there is value in the language he was taught at home, but also in the skill of being able to use professional academic vocabulary when needed. After Jesse practiced his interview skills and thought methodically about the language he was utilizing in the interview, he became one of the sub shop's best sandwich makers. We can say this with confidence, as we had lunch at least once a week with Jesse as our chef!

The Power of Language

The more students read, the more they develop a rich vocabulary. Even after controlling for general intelligence, reading volume significantly contributes to vocabulary knowledge (Cunningham & Stanovich, 2001). Written vocabulary is also important because oral language uses a much smaller vocabulary than written language. Students must be exposed to challenging text to increase their vocabulary, as almost all rare words are gained from print (Cunningham & Stanovich, 2001).

As lifetime educators, we have been amazed by the variability of students' vocabulary. Brianne remembers when a seventh-grade class was reading an excerpt from *To Kill a Mockingbird*. Dill had run away from home and hidden under Scout's bed. Brianne asked the students to describe, in one word, what they thought Dill was feeling at that moment. Betsy raised her hand quickly and blurted out, "Sad!" Ben provided the word "unwanted," and Muli answered "alienated." While all the students were accurate in their responses, the *tier* of each word was thought-provoking. Beck, McKeown, and Kucan (2013) classify words as follows:

Tier 1 These are the common, everyday words that most children enter school knowing already. Since we don't need to teach these, this is a tier without tears!

Tier 2 This tier consists of words that are used across the content areas and are important for students to know and understand. Included here are process words like *analyze* and *evaluate* that students will run into on many standardized tests and that are also used at the university level, in many careers, and in everyday life. We really want to get these words into students' long-term memory. We also advocate adding core values like honesty, resilience, and empathy. Even though students may hear these words, teaching them explicitly and reflecting on their meaning is critical.

Tier 3 This tier consists of content-specific vocabulary—the words that are often defined in textbooks or glossaries. These words are important for imparting ideas during lessons and helping to build students' background knowledge.

So what exactly contributes to vocabulary knowledge and acquisition? We would like to think it's our amazing teaching skills that will expand our students' lingo, but, alas, many argue that our stellar teaching practices alone are not the sole contributor. Hart and Risley (1995) established that the "vocabulary of children from families with low economic status develops at a slower pace than that of children from high economic status." Many researchers have established a correlation between vocabulary and socioeconomic status (Bradley & Corwyn, 2002; Hart & Risley, 1995). This doesn't mean that students from lower-income families can't build the same level of vocabulary, nor should this research create deficit-based views about what students are capable of. Rather, it helps us to predict variability in prior knowledge of Tier 2 and Tier 3 words so that we can help students to build language. We can't simply hand out a list of new words and definitions, which, sadly, was the way that many of us were taught.

As we reflected on vocabulary instruction and how we acquire language, Brianne shared her experience from junior high. Each morning, her awkward junior high self would enter Mrs. Hatch's seventh-grade language arts class, and without fail the "Word of the Day"' would be up on the chalkboard and the Webster's dictionaries would be stacked for everyone to grab on the way in. Like well-trained soldiers, students grabbed a dictionary, sat down at their desks, and began the daily mundane task of "look up the word in the dictionary, write the definition, and use it in a sentence." Then they would all share out. This inevitably took up a good third of the class period, but they had learned a new word! Or had they?

Somewhere along the way, teachers assumed that if we color-coded our notes and they were consolidated into one college-ruled notebook, we would retain all the information. This was definitely not the case. Starting each class armed with a clearly used Webster's dictionary and gel pens representing every color of the rainbow does not a wordsmith make.

Without opportunities for students to discuss the word, explore visuals of it, create a nonlinguistic representation of it, or be introduced to it in context, vocabulary instruction is often a mundane task with little benefit. (Although, if we're keeping it real, there's some sense of accomplishment from creating an organized notebook bedazzled in the colors of the rainbow. In regards to vocabulary instruction, not so much.)

Admittedly, as early teachers, we too followed some of these traditional vocabulary activities. However, as we began to realize that our students couldn't remember the word they had learned the day or two before, we began to delve a bit deeper into vocabulary teaching practices.

A goal of the Institute of Educational Sciences (IES) is to publish practice guides with evidence-based recommendations to support educators in improving literacy levels. A practice guide from 2008 places a strong emphasis on providing explicit vocabulary instruction. So how do we integrate that into units grounded in student voice and diverse text sets?

There isn't a one-size-fits-all method for teaching vocabulary, nor would we want one! This is the beauty of our career; teachers get to work their magic based on the culture of their classrooms. One must consider a student's background, experiences, and interests when diving into the depths of vocabulary instruction. But it helps to start with a framework for language instruction and then take it from there.

For this chapter, we'll dive into vocabulary instruction based on a text set unit using *Long Way Down* by Jason Reynolds. *Long Way Down* follows the story of Will, a 15-year-old boy who has lost his older brother to gun violence. Let's examine how to design meaningful vocabulary instruction through the lens of UDL and develop strategies for integrating ongoing work in social-emotional learning, character education, and restorative practices.

As a first step in this unit, we selected vocabulary words in all three tiers to ensure that students had access to generalized vocabulary, vocabulary focused on core values and character traits, and domain-specific vocabulary that would support them as we read the novel. Table 6-1 identifies vocabulary words that were selected to ground the unit of study. In addition to these words, we encouraged students to create their own vocabulary lists based on words they were not familiar with.

Table 6-1. Vocabulary Words From *Long Way Down,* by Jason Reynolds

Tier 1 words	Tier 2 words	Tier 3 words
Self-awareness	Perpetrator	Flashbacks
Empathy	Redemption	Foreshadowing
Grief	Resilience	Imagery
Descent	Trepidation	Stream of consciousness
Despair	Vendetta	Symbolism
	Vigilante	

Selecting vocabulary words that support social-emotional learning, character education, and restorative practices is important because it helps educators create a more holistic learning experience for their students. By incorporating vocabulary words that promote these values into their novel studies, educators can help students better understand and internalize these concepts.

For example, in *Long Way Down*, selecting words like *self-awareness*, *empathy*, *grief*, *descent*, and *despair* can help students better understand the emotional experiences of the characters in the book. These words can also help students build their own social-emotional skills, such as self-awareness and empathy, by encouraging them to reflect on their own feelings and those of others.

Empathy is a particularly important concept for character development and restorative practices because it encourages students to approach relationships with compassion and understanding. When students understand the perspectives and emotions of others, they are better able to resolve conflicts and build strong, positive relationships. This, in turn, can help create a more supportive and inclusive learning environment.

Selecting vocabulary words that align with restorative practices can also help reinforce key values such as accountability, respect, and responsibility while building shared language and understanding. When students learn to take responsibility for their actions, communicate effectively, and show respect and empathy toward others, they are better equipped to navigate interpersonal challenges and contribute positively to their learning communities.

Systematic Academic Vocabulary Instruction

One helpful framework is SAVI, or Systematic Academic Vocabulary Instruction. SAVI is a vocabulary teaching method based upon the teachings of Robert Marzano's (2004) book, *Building*

Background Knowledge for Academic Achievement. We'll use this six-step process to explicitly teach the word *empathy*, an important component of social-emotional learning and a core value of many schools and districts:

1. Describe, Describe, Describe.

Foster student self-reflection as they discuss any prior knowledge of the word. As students discuss what they know about the word *empathy*, listen for misconceptions and mispronunciations. It is important to remember that modeling pronunciation is often not enough for multilingual learners if they mispronounce something; this is the time to pronounce the term for them and have them practice saying the word aloud. In addition, provide students with stories, descriptions, explanations, and visual or multimedia examples of the concept of empathy. This step is a perfect place to use Guided Language Acquisition Design (GLAD) picture-file cards, observation charts, and even input charts. Using multiple means of representation provides students with a nonlinguistic representation of new terms. This will assist with initial understanding and also support students' ability to create their own visuals later on. It is critical to remember that we don't start by providing students with definitions. Saying to students, "Empathy is the ability to sense other people's emotions, coupled with the ability to imagine what someone else might be thinking or feeling," as an entry point may hamper their own background knowledge. The most natural way for anyone to learn new vocabulary is first to learn in an organic, general way. Most people don't start learning new terms with formal definitions. So keep it simple.

2. Discuss, Discuss, Discuss.

This is the step where elements of English language development (ELD) are really evident. What better way to develop language than to use language? During step 2, students dominate the conversation in the classroom; provide opportunities for them to state their initial understanding of the term *empathy*. Students are encouraged to make connections between the term and familiar situations or current events. GLAD strategies effective during step 2 include the Cognitive Content Dictionary (CCD), recall of your input chart, a process grid, and the easy-to-use 10/2. These strategies, as well as student conversation and discussion that occurs during step 2 in the SAVI program, provide the teacher with opportunities for informal assessment. It is during these discussions that the teacher can monitor student responses.

3. **Draw, Draw, Draw.**

   Step 3 students are asked to construct a picture, image, symbol, video, or sketch representing the term. This would be a great opportunity to integrate students' love of social media! Imagine a series of TikTok videos focused on empathy! In addition to including a description of the term and assessing their own understanding of the term, the research supports using nonlinguistic (imagery-based) activities along with language-based activities to anchor information in permanent memory. Giving students opportunities to share their images with partners, in small groups, or individually with the teacher supports their understanding and encourages the use of vocabulary, which in turn creates the opportunity for them to participate in the academic discourse.

4. **Engage, Engage, Engage.**

   Engage students in learning that provides an opportunity to deepen their knowledge of the terms. Share authentic examples in writing, and provide word banks to empower students to integrate the language into their writing and discussions. For example, a word bank to support discussions about empathy could include compassion, awareness, consideration, openness, listening, and support. Additionally, you could share a text set of songs and the visuals from step 3 that depict empathy. For example, the lyrics of these songs from popular artists represent the concept of empathy:

- "Epiphany" by Taylor Swift
- "Tin Man" by Miranda Lambert
- "Doo Wop (That Thing)" by Lauryn Hill
- "Umbrella" by Rihanna

Sharing the lyrics and music videos would help students to connect to the concept of empathy using multiple means of representation. All of these activities allow for extended development of student understanding.

5. **Partner/Group Discussion.**

Encourage students to continue their discussion about empathy with one another using the visuals, word bank, and song lyrics, or other examples. This deepens their understanding. During this step, it is important to remember to give students a specific task before asking them to engage in discussion. Using prompts, sentence stems, and modeling works well to focus discussions and provides opportunities for authentic, informal assessment of language. For example, "Discuss a time when someone showed you empathy and how that impacted you." You could share your own story of empathy and provide a sentence frame like, "Once when I was feeling _____, someone showed me empathy by _____. This made me feel _____."

6. Games, Games, Games.

Games provide an instructional tool that can keep terms in the forefront of students' thinking while energizing the learning situation. A couple of the games mentioned in Pickering and Marzano's (2005) *Building Academic Vocabulary* include:

- **Pictionary:** Students draw a term for their team.
- **Vocabulary Charades:** Students act out the terms using gestures and body movements.

What's especially exciting about these games is that there are literally multiple digital versions of each out there for us to use. Given the explosion of educational technology and ease of use, this final step of "games" is limitless!

When our team originally brainstormed the SAVI steps, we kept it simple. Students today can collectively create Pictionary games with students around the world. Virtual conference platforms provide the opportunity to bring a classroom of students working on the same vocabulary terms in Jamaica together with students from the United States. Anyone who has ever tried to learn a new language will tell you that the best way to learn it is to use it. We're slightly embarrassed to admit our jealousy of our students today and their ability to practice language with students from around the globe—literally in the comfort of their own home! What an upgrade from our pen pals. We'll get over it.

Here we've discussed the SAVI process with the word *empathy*, but you can complete the process with a set of words instead of teaching them individually. Additionally, you can incorporate extended prompts using some of the target vocabulary words. One of the other target vocabulary words in *Long Way Down* is *self-awareness*, which is an important skill in social-emotional learning and a core value.

After teaching students about self-awareness using the six-step method, we created a character-based writing prompt. In true UDL form, students can choose how they will submit their response (e.g., write a journal entry, record a video response, or create a nonlinguistic representation or drawing). The beauty of choice is that students can meet the objective or demonstrate understanding in multiple ways! Take a minute to check out the following student sample:

Character Prompt: *Long Way Down* by Jason Reynolds

Self-awareness is defined as conscious knowledge of one's own character, feelings, motives, and desires. Take a look at what the characters experience in today's reading. Do you relate to any part of their journey? Be sure to cite evidence from today's reading in your response to the following questions.

- Why is being self-aware an important character trait?
- Do you think you have good self-awareness? Why or why not?

Student Response

In my opinion being self-aware is very important even as you're growing up. Today we read about the ghost of Will's best friend, Dani. She was killed when they were kids by a stray bullet from a gang shooting. The same thing happened on my street when I was younger. To be honest, it has happened more than once. I can almost relate to the book itself, living in a dangerous community can be tricky but being self-aware helps a lot. You always have to be aware of your surroundings and of your doings. Being self-aware helps your intuition to never hang out with the wrong crowds and to just keep moving forward. Living in a neighborhood where gangs are actually a thing, I think for most part my self-awareness really plays the part in my life. I wish I could say the same for a lot of people but I know my own character and I want big things in life. So yes I think being self-aware is really good trait to have.

Essential Questions for Examining Vocabulary

Having an essential question for each unit can also help to craft meaningful prompts for discussion and writing and provides opportunities for students to continually reflect on new vocabulary. Incorporating your vocabulary words into meaningful essential questions can help create purpose for units of study. According to McTighe and Wiggins (2013), essential questions have seven characteristics. They:

- Are open-ended
- Are thought provoking
- Require higher-order thinking
- Point toward big transferable ideas
- Raise additional questions
- Require justification
- Recur over time

McTighe and Wiggins also assert that many different types of questions meet the first six criteria. However, the challenge is creating an essential question that recurs over time. Let's take a look at an essential question for *Long Way Down.* "What does empathy mean to you?" begs students to examine daily readings and discussion and reflect back upon their own lived experiences. The purpose of the essential question is to connect students' lives and experiences to the characters and people they study, and we argue that we can incorporate target vocabulary into the essential questions.

Archer's Story

As we were teaching vocabulary through the SAVI method, it also became apparent how different students' life experiences would contribute to the outcome of the term's meaning for that student. He was wise and mature beyond his years, and his life experiences had forced him to endure tragedies that no 15-year-old should experience. As a class, we were reading an informational article and the word *nefarious* was mentioned multiple times in context.

So, the six-step process began. Archer was rather quiet and wasn't demonstrating a clear understanding of the word. Then came the few moments of independent time to draw a symbol, term, or picture of what this word means and a way for him to assess his own understanding of the term. We walked around the room and peeked at each student's paper. We stopped abruptly at Archer's side and were taken aback by his art. Our first thought was, *Wow, that's a super-detailed drawing*, immediately followed by, *Well, that's a bit disturbing.* Archer had drawn a very detailed picture of a person lying face down on the ground while another stood over him, stabbing him repeatedly.

We asked, "Archer, what are we looking at?"

Archer replied in his mature, confident voice, "A nefarious action. You see, that's my homeboy on the ground and the nefarious person stabbing him is his dad."

We have never forgotten this word or memory, and we would bet that Archer can still tell you today the meaning of *nefarious.*

When we select meaningful vocabulary terms in all three tiers and provide opportunities for students to use the language as they read, write, speak, and listen, we can create spaces for students to bring their funds of knowledge, contribute to the classroom community, and create a space of shared, authentic learning. Teaching vocabulary in such a way will also aid students in their comprehension of complex text.

Reflection Questions

1. All of us have one powerful lesson we learned in our careers that we like to share about student expression. The "vernacular" story was Jina's memorable share-out story. What was yours? If you're a social media user, share your wisdom with other teachers at #UDLNowELA.

2. If you had the chance to redesign your experience and create your own method of vocabulary instruction, what does that look like? Be specific!

3. How does the tiered vocabulary chart for *Long Way Down* help you visualize the importance of creating your own vocabulary chart for a unit of study?

4. Reflecting on Archer's story, how will you build on a student's funds of knowledge and incorporate them into your vocabulary instructional design?

7

The Power of Authentic Writing

Frosting Before Cake

Brianne Parker

As a young child, I always had a passion for writing. My love began with the stories that my five-year-old self would create on folded, lined paper. I would create these books for anyone and everyone who would acknowledge and encourage my craft. I would spend hours writing and creating. I could get lost in my own imagination and augmented reality, and it became an escape. I wrote about everything—my dog, going shopping, my best friend, and even how unfair my older sister, Autumn, could be. I remember my grandmother, also my biggest fan, asking me why there were never any illustrations to accompany my writings. Grandma would always say, "The pictures are just the frosting on the cake!" To me, the words on the page created more than what a picture could possibly ever depict. The power of words was immeasurable in my eyes. Still, I would create the pictures to accompany my text simply because Grandma found joy in my stick-figure art.

Fast-forward 20 years, and I was teaching high school students, namely at-promise youth. I still held a love for words and writing, but time had altered my relationship with my craft. I was no longer writing for whoever would read, but specifically for a purpose and to encourage my often-resistant students to find their imaginative and authentic selves through writing. My goal and hope was that my students would lose themselves in the words that created worlds where only they could truly find comfort and belonging.

I hung up a lot of posters with an abundance of vocabulary words, a description of the writing process, and even parts of speech, because clearly these posters were going to encourage my students (ha!). The first time Jina walked into my class, she looked around at all the posters I had so proudly hung on my walls and raised her eyebrows. "Wow, I would hate your classroom. There are a lot of words on your wall. Where are all the pictures, the visuals?"

My soul was crushed; my love affair with writing had just been smashed, stomped. She continued, "What about kids like me? We need to read and be able to visualize. I need color!" It was then that I realized that maybe the words were the best part of the cake, but some needed the frosting too. Students need visuals, exemplars, and support.

Several years later, I welcomed my first daughter, Clare, into the world. As she entered kindergarten, we would practice writing simple sentences such as "I walked my dog" or "I like cookies." Clare often became frustrated with formulating the syntax, but she was very artistic and would draw, paint, and create on anything she could find . . . even my walls. I thought back to my grandmother's words and Jina's insight and had the epiphany of the frosting before the cake. Why not? From that point forward, Clare would start most creative writing assignments with a picture. Even today, as a high schooler, she'll doodle with purpose before writing in her honors English class. For her, the frosting was before the cake.

Although these conversations may sound silly or simple, it was an "aha" for me in my journey as an educator. For some, writing begins as a collection of words that create and depict one's imaginative and realistic style of writing. However, for others, like Jina and Clare, the writing process begins with an image or visual, and the words follow. Recognizing that there isn't a single strategy or process that works for everyone has changed the way I support students in their writing lives.

Harnessing the Power of Multiple Tasks and Formats

The novel *Refugee*, by Alan Gratz, is impactful not only because it juxtaposes the historical journeys of three young refugees, but also because it presents the opportunity to explore many varied styles of writing. Students are required in the CCSS ELA high school grade 9–10 standards to "write informative/explanatory texts to examine and convey complex ideas, concepts, and information clearly and accurately through the effective selection, organization, and analysis of content." Students are challenged not only to examine and describe their texts, but also to establish real-life connections. Several years ago, before we learned about UDL, students were provided the following prompt:

> Characters in literature often have a strong impact on us because they change and grow throughout the book or play. In this assignment, you will write a 5-paragraph essay on a memorable character of your choice from the novel *Refugee* by Alan Gratz. Include sufficient detail and strong support in your review.
>
> 1. Describe in detail a memorable character.
>
> 2. Explain how and why the character grew/changed and what impact the character had on you.
>
> 3. Describe characteristics that you appreciated, disapproved of, and/or found interesting.

Although our expectations were that the students would submit a standard essay addressing these points, Ronald, a seemingly quiet boy who was rather new to the class, approached us after class with a request.

"Can I write a poem? What I mean is answer all these questions, but write it in a poem? I love to write poetry."

We had never really thought that this sort of assignment could be completed in a way other than an analytical/opinion five-paragraph essay, but Ronald forced the norm to be expanded. Not only did Ronald answer all aspects of the prompt, but he opened our eyes to the prospect that genres do not have to be taught in isolation or specifically in a "unit of study." Ronald's interest was overflowing, and so was his buy-in. The following year, Ronald's influence changed the assignment directions to:

> Characters in literature often have a strong impact on us because they change and grow throughout the book or play. In this assignment, you will create a written product on a memorable character of your choice from the novel *Refugee*. Include sufficient detail and strong support in your review. Choose the genre of writing of your choice: essay, poem, song, etc. Be sure all questions are answered in your response and that you cite evidence from the text.

Through Ronald's desire to push the boundaries of educational creativity, he and other students were given the opportunity to "write informative/explanatory texts to examine and convey complex ideas, concepts, and information clearly and accurately through the effective selection, organization, and analysis of content" using various writing genres—without losing the importance of the writing process.

Moving Beyond Five Paragraphs

As an ELA teacher, you are constantly balancing instruction in reading comprehension, vocabulary development, speaking and listening, and writing. Throughout this text, we've discussed how to ground units of study in high-quality texts, grade-level standards, and essential questions that focus on building social-emotional learning and character. Although it's valuable for students to have options to share their understanding of text using multiple means of action and expression, we're all firmly in the camp that sometimes students have to write. When working on content standards, we can provide students with options and choices for how they share their learning, but when we're working on writing—well, that's that. As much as it's valuable for students to connect with one another, have face-to-face conversations, and use innovative multimedia technology to communicate, writing is still a critical skill.

Many students are taught from early in their education that a "good essay" is composed of five paragraphs: an introduction, three body paragraphs, and a conclusion. We are all guilty of the same practice! That's the way many of us learned to write. If we had a nickel for every time we heard "five-paragraph essay," we'd be rich. First, to be clear, there is a 5-paragraph essay, but there's also a 4-paragraph, 17-paragraph, and 22-paragraph essay. The number of paragraphs isn't as important as whether the writing is organized appropriately for the task.

Our standards require us to move away from counting paragraphs and instead teach students to focus on the task, the intended audience, and the purpose of writing. Sometimes it's appropriate to address a prompt using five paragraphs, but there's no rule that essays are bound to a scripted format or paragraph count. In fact, the predictable structure may actually decrease student cognitive engagement.

Kimberly Hill Campbell (2014) is the chair of teacher education at the Lewis and Clark Graduate School. In her essay "Beyond the Five-Paragraph Essay," she writes:

> *Having taught the five-paragraph formula to high school students, I recognize its appeal. It appears to offer a way*

> into writing for students who need help in organizing their thoughts. As I sat down to write this article for Educational Leadership, I found myself wishing for a formula I could turn to to help me organize my thinking—to find a way in.
>
> But this is the problem with the five-paragraph formula; its offer of structure stops the very thinking we need students to do. Their focus becomes fitting sentences into the correct slots rather than figuring out for themselves what they're trying to say and the best structure for saying it.

Writing is an art. It is valuable to start with a predictable formula, but then we have to provide scaffolding to encourage students to explore other ways of writing. Great writers don't follow formulas. What sets them apart is their own voice, their style, and sometimes even their bastardization of the rules of grammar (we chose our vernacular purposefully there for effect!). Wherever you start with students, be sure to provide scaffolding so they know that a five-paragraph essay, the graphic organizer, or the predictable outline is just a starting point and not a rule. Ronald moved away from the five-paragraph essay because he knew he could address the task in a more authentic way with a different format.

We need to focus on firm goals and flexible means when it comes to writing instruction. If we don't teach this flexibility, "the importance, versatility, and pervasiveness of writing exacts a toll on those who do not learn to write well, as this can limit academic, occupational, and personal attainments" (Graham, 2019). Hyper-focusing on one style of writing may limit a student's access to the versatile writing that is needed to be adaptable to life situations. However, creating a foundation of solid writing skills will help any student become a better writer. Access to various styles of writing—such as fiction, nonfiction, journals, rap lyrics, magazines, letters, and interviews—will broaden students' knowledge of styles of writing and grow their craft. Exposure to various writing genres will only support a student's writing development.

One challenge of writing instruction is clearly articulated by the Institute of Education Sciences (2018):

> *Assessing writing is a fundamentally subjective judgment and depends at least in part on the framework the reader brings to the task. Despite the subjective nature of writing assessment, there are some features that many can agree contribute to effective writing (e.g., following basic language conventions so a reader is able to interpret the text's meaning or developing a clear focus for the reader). In order to address some of the inherent subjectivity of writing measures, the panel included only outcomes for which the researchers demonstrated that multiple raters could evaluate the same students' work consistently. Exceptions were given to norm-referenced standardized tests and a small number of measures that were more objective (e.g., word count).*

Given this research, we strongly advocate working with your PLC to create interrater reliability so you have a clear and consistent vision, with clear success criteria and multiple exemplars, to ensure students have the best chance of building their writing voice even when they're choosing different formats for writing.

Calibrating "Good" Writing

Although rubrics are valuable for both teachers and students to identify mastery criteria, there are two potential errors that can lead to very different assessments using the same rubric. Becoming familiar with these sources of error and following a protocol to minimize them will enhance the capacity of all teachers to reliably assess student work and provide mastery-oriented feedback in universally designed classrooms. Sometimes, our assessment of student writing isn't accurate because of the interactions between students and us as raters. When teachers know students well, they sometimes predict how students will perform on a task. These predictions can subconsciously affect scoring. We are also navigating the interactions between raters and tasks. Educators sometimes have different interpretations of a task and therefore are expecting different responses. We have to work in our PLCs to reduce the bias in assessing writing and providing feedback. We can do so if we use student writing and complete interrater reliability protocols. The following steps may be valuable:

1. Before reading student responses, discuss the prompt and the type of response that would be necessary for a complete, clear, and accurate answer. This discussion will minimize errors based on the interactions between raters and the task.

2. After this discussion, the first response is selected and read by each teacher.

3. After each rater has recorded their mark, the marks are revealed.

4. If there is a difference in the scores assigned, a discussion begins. In this case, raters describe their rationales for the marks they have given and reach a consensus. Once a consensus is reached, that paper becomes the anchor paper, or the exemplar, for that scoring category.

5. Teachers can then use those exemplars as they assess all remaining student papers. This helps to get everyone on the same page and also provides a set of exemplars to students.

The What Works Clearinghouse, a project of the Institute of Educational Sciences, publishes practice guides to support the implementation of evidence-based practices. Recommendations for supporting student writing include the following (IES, 2019):

- Explicitly teach appropriate writing strategies using a Model-Practice-Reflect instructional cycle.

- Use assessments of student writing to inform instruction and feedback.

Each of these recommendations aligns with the work of UDL, and the type of learning environment we've been advocating for, by integrating multiple frameworks. We will discuss these recommendations in more detail in the sections that follow.

Practicing Model-Practice-Reflect

Once we determine what "good" writing looks like, we have to model that. When we teach high-quality texts, we have models of effective writing at our fingertips, but it's also important for students to see their peers' writing, aligned to the mastery of grade-level standards. So what are some tools and scaffolds to support students' success in writing through the lens of UDL?

Exemplars

Imagine providing students with a rubric to score an informative writing piece. Students are provided with not only the rubric but also examples of written artifacts that are scored according to the various levels of the rubric. Students are taught the importance of writing skills and the requirements of strong writing. Table 7-1 shows the criteria for mastery for the selection and citation of evidence on the informative/explanatory writing rubric from the Literacy Design Collaborative (2018).

Through reading, editing, and examining the written artifacts, students are given the opportunity to understand the process and expectations prior to being required to demonstrate mastery of the objective. The use of exemplars provides students with an in-depth example of the assignment expectations. They will benefit not only from seeing that they meet the desired outcomes, but also from seeing other narratives that may fall short. This may seem like a lot of work to find the exemplars, but worry not: The chatbots can help with that. We shared the rubric in Table 7-1 with ChatGPT and asked it to create an example of writing for each category. What an awesome way to use this technology!

Table 7-1. Informational/Explanatory Rubric for Grades 9-12 Teaching Tasks

	Emerging	Approaches expectations	Meets expectations	Advanced
Selection and citation of evidence	Includes minimal details from sources. Sources are used without citation.	Includes details, examples, and/or quotations from sources that are relevant to the controlling idea. Inconsistently cites sources.	Includes details, examples, and/or quotations from sources that support the controlling and supporting ideas. Consistently cites sources with minor formatting errors.	Includes well-chosen details, examples, and/or quotations from sources that fully support the controlling and supporting ideas. Consistently cites sources using appropriate format.

Here are the exemplar and explanation for the lowest level of performance, "Not yet":

To ChatGPT: Could you write an example of a response for the book *Refugee* by Alan Gratz that is the lowest level of performance?

ChatGPT: Sure, here's an example of a response for the same prompt that would be considered the lowest level of performance according to the rubric criteria:

"In *Refugee*, there are many memorable characters. One of them is Mahmoud, a young Syrian boy who is forced to flee his home country. Throughout the book, Mahmoud faces many challenges and grows as a character. He shows bravery and compassion, and he learns to adapt to his new surroundings."

This response may attempt to present information in response to the prompt, but it lacks connections or relevance to the prompt's purpose. The prompt asks the writer to choose a memorable character from the novel and analyze how that character changes and grows throughout the book. This response simply summarizes the basic plot points related to Mahmoud without offering any details, examples, or quotations, nor an analysis or insight into how his character changes or why he is memorable.

Think about what a timesaver it is to create exemplars that way! And believe us, we know that it's hard work to create these scaffolds. Brianne's son had a teacher who believed in grading an essay on what she "felt" it had earned. Brianne's son was confused by the expectations and requirements of various writing assignments and asked for a rubric or example of the expected outcome for his writing assignments. The teacher was unable to produce either. Exemplars would have provided clarity to both the learner and educator. The use of exemplars is a standard that all educators should explore in order to provide opportunities for their students to understand exceptionality. And again, the chatbots can help! Although we only provided an example for the lowest level of performance, you can generate examples that meet and exceed the criteria for mastery, or better yet, have the students generate the exemplars themselves! Providing students with a tangible example of the expectation gives them a solid foundation and helps eliminate "How do I write that?" and "What does that look like?" confusion.

After clearly sharing success criteria and exemplars, it is important that we as educators identify the predictable barriers that may prevent students from writing well. In an inclusive classroom, you can predict that some students will struggle with organization, word choice, or sentence structure. Given this, it's critical that we not only share numerous examples of effective writing but also ensure that all students have the scaffolds they need to create writing where they express what they know with voice, style, and clarity.

As you think about writing instruction through the UDL lens, the following scaffolds may support students who need additional support.

Sentence Frames

Sentence frames are ready-to-use language building blocks. They help learners express their ideas clearly without having to worry about proper grammar. There are two types of sentence frames: closed and open. *Closed frames* are highly structured, usually prompting only for a word or phrase, and may appear as limiting. *Open frames* also provide structure and support, but they allow ample room for creativity and growth as well. A closed frame example might be, "In the book *Refugee*, I chose the character_____. I would describe this character as _____ and _____." As you can see, the frame appears to be more of a fill-in-the-blank exercise than a tool for creative expression.

Open frames, as the name implies, are more open-ended, such as "In the book *Refugee*, the character that made the greatest impression on me was _____ because _____" or "When I read _____, I immediately connected to the character because _____."

Let's examine a student story where chatbot technology could help to generate sentence stems. While reading *Refugee*, Amir, a student in Brianne's ELA class, related to all three characters in that his first language was not English. Amir entered school in the United States around the age of 15. His family had fled Iran due to social unrest and found refuge in China when he was just 4 years old. Amir's academic journey has been nothing short of rigorous; however, as he entered an American high school at the age of 15 with incomplete English fluency, he struggled to keep up with his classmates. Amir wanted to engage in the rich academic content, but he struggled due to language barriers.

Amir's motivation to acquire the English language was off the charts, but he struggled with how to organize writing and often requested exemplars before he drafted his own work. As we wrote this chapter, we imagined how beneficial it would have been if ChatGPT had been available to Amir.

To ChatGPT

I want to write a response about how I connect with characters in a book. Can you share some sentence frames that will help me?

From ChatGPT

- The character's experiences resonated with me because _____.
- The character's journey made me reflect on my own experiences of _____.
- I could relate to the character's feelings of _____.
- I identified with the character's struggles to _____.
- I felt a strong connection to the character when the _____.
- I could understand the character's motivations when the _____.

Boom! Sentence stems done!

Graphic Organizers

Graphic organizers are tools that provide learners with a visual representation of information, concepts, and ideas. Graphic organizers are easy to create and impactful in simplifying information. Additionally, they may support the development of cognitive skills such as brainstorming, critical and creative thinking, categorizing and prioritizing content, reflection, and more.

Assessing Writing to Inform Reflection and Feedback

Ernest Hemingway said that the scariest thing he ever encountered was "a blank piece of paper." In a universally designed ELA classroom, we can leverage numerous collaboration and feedback mechanisms throughout the writing process to minimize that threat.

Early in our educational journeys, we all learned the five basic steps of the writing process: prewriting, drafting, revising, editing, and publishing. We must admit that, although these steps are valuable for developing a well-written product, we may not have always followed them just as they were intended. Some of these steps may have been missed, while others were repeated, over and over and over again—especially the revision piece.

Revise, revise, revise—you're never really done revising! Brianne still sees her college professor standing at the podium, shaking the stack of freshly graded papers and repeating this chant. But what truly is revision? Is it just *one* step in the process? We argue that it isn't. We can revise at every step in the process. Revision is a continuous process that is driven by feedback and reflection. We can support student reflection and optimize feedback by incorporating writing conferences, peer review, and student self-reflection.

Conferencing provides an opportunity for the writer and reader to discuss the composition in progress. Essentially, conferencing is a conversation between the reader and the writer, which aren't always the student and teacher—we can also schedule conferences between and among students. You could even create a circle for students to share a short excerpt of their writing where they would appreciate feedback. Regardless of how you schedule conferences, they're an opportunity for authentic connection, exploration, feedback, and reflection.

In her piece "Using Conferences to Support the Writing Process," Betsy Bowen (1993) suggests that "effective conferences are characterized by reversible role relationships [and] provide the opportunity to discuss both process and product, offer writers attuned support, and provide a predictable structure for writers."

So where does conferencing belong in the writing process: in the beginning, middle, or end? We believe it should go wherever it is needed and can be utilized multiple times throughout the process.

Peer Review

Ah, peer review. It can be so, so good, but it can be so, so . . . well, an exercise in frustration. Worry not: Research is clear that with training, guidance, and practice, students can learn to be more specific and helpful in their responses to a peer's writing (Eksi, 2012).

In our experience with having students peer review each other's writings, students respond, "Great job" not because the writing is great, but because that's the quickest and easiest feedback to provide or because the simple prospect of providing feedback drags them into the abyss of confusion. As with all UDL practices, we need to scaffold effective peer review in the writing process (see Table 7-2).

Table 7-2. Peer Feedback Choice Board (Tucker & Novak, 2022)

Directions: Select TWO prompts from the peer feedback choice board to provide your classmate with specific, meaningful, and kind feedback. Capture your feedback in the space below the choice board!	
Greatest strength	**Tiny tweaks**
Identify the strongest aspect of this assignment. What specifically was strong? Why do you think this element was particularly powerful or well done? How did this element positively impact the overall quality of this work?	Identify one aspect of this assignment that would benefit from a minor adjustment, modification, or tweak. What would you suggest the student rework or reimagine? How would reworking this element impact the overall quality of this work? Do you have specific recommendations for how they might improve this aspect of their work?

Table 7-2 Continued. Peer Feedback Choice Board (Tucker & Novak, 2022)

Directions: Select TWO prompts from the peer feedback choice board to provide your classmate with specific, meaningful, and kind feedback. Capture your feedback in the space below the choice board!

Celebrate surprises

As you reviewed this assignment, what surprised you about this student's work? Was there an aspect of their work that was unexpected, original, outside of the box, engaging, or thought-provoking? Describe why you liked this aspect of their work.

Hungry for more

Identify a part of this assignment that needs further development. What would you have enjoyed knowing more about or having more information on? Where could more detail and development have strengthened this? Can you identify the specific places in this assignment where the student should spend time digging deeper?

Mind blown

Identify something in this assignment that you loved and had not considered as you completed your work. Is there a great idea or approach that this student used to complete this assignment that you would like to incorporate into your work? Why did you like this element of their draft? How can you incorporate this idea or approach into your work?

Clarifying confusion

As you reviewed this assignment, was there anything unclear, confusing, or that left you wondering? Is there an aspect of this draft that you would like clarity on or more specifics about? Were any of the steps or statements unclear? Can you identify specific elements of this assignment that would benefit from clearer language or more explanation?

Record your feedback below in writing, a short video, or an audio recording. Please be specific and kind.

In *Shift to Student-Led*, Katie and Catlin Tucker (2022) discuss the importance of empowering students to provide each other with feedback. They note, "Building student agency into the peer-feedback process removes barriers and encourages students to provide feedback through a specific lens. Based on what a student sees in the work they are reviewing, they may be drawn to one option on the choice board over another."

Peer review can be effective not only for the writer but also for the reviewer. Giving feedback or opinions on a peer's topic can be useful in generating more ideas and purposes to include within the text. Similarly, the reviewer is exposed to new ideas and writing styles.

 Peer review is a strategy that aligns beautifully with UDL, social-emotional learning, character education, and restorative practices. By participating in peer review, students have the opportunity to build relationships with their peers and to practice skills such as empathy, communication, and respect to reinforce core values and character traits that are critical for success in relationships and life. Peer review can also help promote self-awareness and reflection as students are asked to consider their own writing and how it might be improved.

Restorative practices, which emphasize accountability and positive relationships, can also be supported through peer review of writing. When students review each other's work, they have the opportunity to practice giving and receiving feedback in a constructive and respectful manner. This can help to build a sense of community and trust within the classroom, as well as support the development of important social and emotional skills.

Self-Assessment

The process of reflection requires ongoing self-assessment, which is a critical social-emotional skill. Writing can't be a one-and-done event. Rather, when we ground writing instruction in meaningful prompts with meaningful texts, we can support our students to explore models, conference with us and their peers, and reflect on peer review. This will help them build their awareness of high-quality writing while also reflecting on their own craft. As with all instructional practices, we have to consider potential barriers and provide the scaffolds and flexibility that students may need to thrive. For example, when students reflect on their writing in comparison to a set of exemplars and success criteria, you may prompt them with the following:

- Why do you give yourself a particular score on the rubric?
- What details in your work support the self-evaluation score you assigned to this piece?
- What does this piece show about your strengths as a student?
- What aspects of this skill or standard are you still working on or struggling with?
- What specific support would help you continue to develop this skill?

Provide options and choices for students to respond in writing, video, or audio or provide opportunities for them to share their self-assessment with classmates as they build in practices that support their social-emotional development. You could also incorporate a prompt like "What does this piece show about your strengths as a student?" in a restorative circle to build a writing community. There are so many ways to incorporate more elements of social-emotional learning, character education, and restorative practices in academic writing instruction.

Reflection Questions

1. How would the interrater reliability protocol help you better understand what "good writing" looks like in your grade and department? How could you adapt the protocol with student writing as they review rubrics and exemplars?

2. Research is clear that writers need numerous opportunities to work through the process of model, practice, and reflect. How do you design opportunities for students to continually go through that process? What are some of the options or choices you provide to ensure that all students have the tools they need to write clearly and express themselves?

3. How can student writing help to create a community of writers through peer review?

4. What are some ways that you support student self-reflection throughout the writing process as students craft meaningful texts by incorporating social-emotional learning and restorative practices?

8

A Focus on Speaking and Listening

The Adopted Daughter of a Retired Nun

Jina Poirier

Let me share a bit about myself as a reference point. Oftentimes, I describe myself as "deliciously average" in every way. I can recall sharing this description of myself during a training for our committee of restorative educators in my district, and it seemed to spark an interesting discussion. To some, this may sound a bit self-deprecating. I actually love and embrace this description of myself, and this is how I choose to identify. Stay with me here . . . I promise there is a point!

We all have a story. The story is a combination of our experiences over time that make up who we are along the way. Outside of being "deliciously average," I was once described by my sassy and brilliant younger sister, Lauren, as the "adopted daughter of a retired nun." Right about now, I have either intrigued or thoroughly confused you! The truth is that both of those descriptions identify parts of me and are pieces to the story that is uniquely *me*. I am adopted, and my mom was in a convent for 14 years prior to adopting me. As for the "deliciously average" description, that one, as I mentioned, is self-reported. Throughout elementary school, my illustrious high school and club volleyball career, and in my family, I would say that I was blessed with being average. I was good at school, not great. On the volleyball court, I could hold my own but was no Misty May-Treanor. I am the youngest of my generation in a vivacious Scotch-Irish family with strong opinions on literally everything, but I am Switzerland: right in the middle!

If I am honest with myself, in school, sports, and home I never felt truly seen or heard. I always felt *loved*, but I could remain quiet and unnoticed if I desired. This is a benefit of being average. I was a chameleon who could blend in easily in multiple crowds.

I would argue that this is the same for many of my students over the last 18 years. If we don't take time to intentionally get to know our students, we lose out on such an epic opportunity. As humans, if we feel seen, heard, and respected, we are involved! The best way to bring this out in our students is to weave the process into their daily activities.

Boyes-Watson and Pranis (2000) share that when we sit in a restorative circle, we are "swimming against the current" of unconscious routines built into the very structure of the school day. As simple as it sounds, changing up the traditional rows of desks and raising our hands to speak can be a powerful community-building tool that fosters speaking and listening. Providing a structured and safe opportunity for all our "deliciously average," amazing students to share their stories is an amazing way to help them bring their true selves into our learning environments. We don't want to miss out on a chance to truly see and know our students. I sometimes wonder what opportunities I missed by not feeling comfortable enough to use my voice.

Utilizing the Social Discipline Window to Honor Voice and Choice

Here we'll introduce the Social Discipline Window to highlight the intersections between voice and choice in UDL, social-emotional learning, and restorative practices. The Social Discipline Window was originally developed by psychologists Stephen Karpman and Bill Harris. However, Paul McCold and Ted Wachtel adapted the model to create the Social Discipline Window for schools.

The adapted model places a greater emphasis on the importance of relationships and community in the school setting. The goal of the Social Discipline Window for schools is to promote positive relationships and collaboration among students, teachers, and administrators. This can be achieved by promoting a culture of respect, communication, and problem-solving.

As illustrated in Figure 8-1, the concept of the Social Discipline Window was adapted to the Four Quadrants of Behavior Support, a framework used in education and behavior management to help teachers understand different approaches to supporting student behavior. The four quadrants are:

To   This quadrant represents a proactive approach to behavior support, where the focus is on teaching and reinforcing positive behavior. This approach emphasizes building positive relationships and creating a supportive learning environment, and may involve using positive reinforcement strategies such as praise and rewards.

With   This quadrant represents a collaborative approach to behavior support, where the focus is on working with students to address challenging behavior. This approach emphasizes listening to and understanding students' perspectives, and may involve using problem-solving and conflict resolution strategies to address behavior issues.

Not This quadrant represents a reactive approach to behavior support, where the focus is on stopping or minimizing negative behavior. This approach may involve using consequences or punishment to discourage unwanted behavior, and may result in a more authoritarian or punitive learning environment.

For This quadrant represents a protective approach to behavior support, where the focus is on providing support and accommodations for students who have more intensive behavior needs. This approach emphasizes individualized support and may involve working with outside professionals to provide specialized services for students who require them.

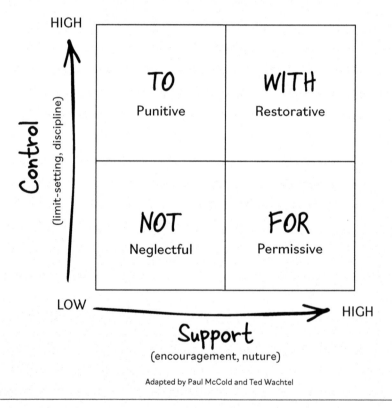

Adapted by Paul McCold and Ted Wachtel

Figure 8-1. Four Quadrants of Behavior Support, adapted from Wachtel & McCold (2000)

By understanding and using the Four Quadrants of Behavior Support, educators can develop a more comprehensive and effective approach to behavior management that addresses the needs of all students in a positive and supportive way.

Students are more inclined to take ownership of their learning when teachers are in the With Restorative corner of the window. Students, and arguably staff as well, are more likely to thrive in an environment where they have a voice. Our entire goal in including restorative practices in our daily curriculum delivery is to honor the power of choice and voice in UDL.

Costello, Wachtel, and Wachtel (2010) assert that the fundamental hypothesis of restorative practices is that "human beings are happier, more cooperative and productive, and more likely to make positive changes in their behavior when those in positions of authority do things WITH them, rather than TO or FOR them." (Costello, Wachtel, & Wachtel, 2010, p. 40). Think about how when we universally design lessons we provide choice and allow for student voice. When students feel as though they are involved and have a say in their learning, there is more engagement. If the goal is to create expert readers and expert learners, students need to be part of our process. It's as if the UDL principles were designed in tandem with restorative practices.

We see restorative circle practice as an authentic way to integrate speaking and listening standards. One of the anchor standards for speaking and listening requires students to prepare for and participate effectively in conversations and collaborations with diverse partners, building on others' ideas and expressing their own clearly and persuasively.

As a teacher, you can integrate this standard throughout your units by setting up restorative circles that ask students to connect to essential questions, share their connections with the text, and listen to each other's ideas in a safe space. In *We Got This*, Cornelius Minor (2018, p. 91) shares the importance of creating a space for students to speak about what they need to be successful. He provides a script that teachers can use to invite feedback:

> I have been thinking lots about the kinds of assignments that I give. I've been struggling with a lot of other teachers, and one of the things that we are learning is that schoolwork is supposed to be something that gives you enough practice at the things that we are learning so that you can get good at them. While you are doing the work today, I'm going to make time for you to talk with the people at your table. There are three things I want you to discuss during that time. I'm putting them on the board:
>
> - How is this assignment helping you to get good at doing this thing independently?
> - How could I change the assignment to make this a better practice experience?
> - Do you know of any materials that you could use that would help you to do this work better?

Consider how prompts like this invite students to become partners in the design and delivery of their literacy experiences. These questions could be posed in a small group or shared in a circle practice. Creating this community also prepares students for more formal presentations, where they share their learning with classmates.

The following speaking and listening standards require students to share their learning using multiple means of representation:

- Integrate and evaluate information presented in diverse media and formats, including visually, quantitatively, and orally.

- Make strategic use of digital media and visual displays of data to express information and enhance understanding of presentations.

A few years ago, one of our amazing social science teachers at Sunburst Youth Academy, Allen, came across a great nonprofit organization called Kiva. Kiva's mission is to provide microloans to underserved communities. People from all over the world, often from poorer countries, submit their proposals to fund their projects. One example is a woman who lives in the Philippines. She was looking to get a loan for $225 dollars to buy feed and other supplies for her pigs. A man in Honduras was looking for a microloan of $225 to help buy fertilizer and mulch for his farm. The people who ask for microloans aren't looking to buy the latest Jordans or a fancy purse, they're just trying to get by.

After learning about what Kiva is, Sunburst staff jumped at the opportunity to teach their cadets about the world outside of the United States. In Allen's inspirational words, it allowed the cadets to become global citizens and show empathy for those less fortunate than them. To increase student engagement, Sunburst made the Kiva project a competition among the cadets. Cadets work in pairs and research someone looking for a microloan. They choose a project that they want to fund, research the country of the person asking for the loan, and determine why the person is asking for the loan. The cadets build a presentation with the information they find and present to a panel of Sunburst staff for the Sunburst Foundation to fund the microloans. On a scale from 1 to 10, Sunburst staff rate cadets on the following:

Research and quality of relevant information The presenters' subject knowledge, quality of research, and use of relevant information

Structure and organization Whether the presenters created a clear, concise, and easy-to-follow presentation that included an introduction and conclusion

Delivery The presenters' public speaking, tone, eye contact, and preparedness

Visual presentation   The presenters' use of technology to create a dynamic, easy-to-read visual aid that showcases the Kiva borrowers they represent

After each team is scored, the top three teams get their projects funded. As of this writing, the Sunburst Foundation has funded $10,000 in microloans.

Why have we chosen to share the Kiva presentations in this discussion of restorative classrooms? It's obvious to us! We happen to know that the classroom Allen runs is a safe space to fail and grow. He provides a space where, if you pay attention, you can literally see the Social Discipline Window in action. Students and staff are developing and creating the presentations together. Technology, paper and pencil, and innovative ideas are all being used. It's not a mystery that students have high anxiety when it comes to public speaking. Having an opportunity to serve others is a dynamic motivator for the students to push through that anxiety. As Mahatma Gandhi said, "The best way to find yourself is to lose yourself in the service of others."

 Authentic project-based learning approaches that involve students speaking and listening to real audiences can provide a variety of benefits in English language arts. These projects can support the development of important social and emotional skills, such as effective communication, collaboration, and self-awareness. When students engage with authentic audiences, they have the opportunity to practice these skills in a real-world context, which can help build confidence and promote social-emotional growth. Additionally, authentic projects can support the development of important character traits, such as empathy, respect, and responsibility. By engaging with diverse audiences, students can learn to appreciate different perspectives and understand the impact of their words and actions on others and the power they have to make a difference in the world around them. Authentic project-based learning strategies also support restorative practices by providing opportunities for students to engage in constructive dialogue and problem-solving with peers and community members. By providing options and choices for students to participate in authentic projects with real audiences, you're building a foundation that can easily integrate UDL, social-emotional learning, character building, and restorative practices.

Reflection Questions

1. How can the Social Discipline Window be used to support student voice and choice in the classroom?

2. How can restorative circles be used to support speaking and listening standards in the classroom?

3. How can the use of prompts and questions in the classroom invite students to become partners in the design and delivery of their literacy experiences?

4. How can you effectively leverage authentic project-based learning experiences, like the Kiva project, to foster speaking and listening skills, social-emotional growth, empathy, and a sense of responsibility among students, ultimately promoting a restorative and inclusive classroom environment?

Conclusion

Opening Up a New World

Anne Wolff

Many people have heard of Harry Potter, the child wizard. Even terms like *Quidditch* and *muggles* have made it into our everyday lexicon. In 1998, while I was sipping a hot chocolate and roaming through Borders bookstore, the intriguing cover art on the new Harry Potter novel caught my attention. Before Harry Potter, I did not enjoy reading and rather thought of it as a chore. I would unenthusiastically read the books required for school, but nothing more. When I came across Harry Potter, my thoughts on reading *changed.*

I devoured the first and second books and could not wait to read the rest of the series. It turns out, I was not alone. I even bought a wand at Universal Studios and used it to keep us all on task while writing this book. Ryan says that it's just a piece of wood, but it seems to be working, so . . . . Anyway, just like millions of young adult readers around the world, I couldn't wait to read the entire series. Much like the *Chronicles of Narnia* series decades before, "the power of the Potter series did more than increase the number of young readers. It so drastically changed preconceived notions about the children's publishing industry that it became known as 'the Harry Potter effect'" (Pierce, 2018).

This series helped to change an entire industry. Local bookstores had midnight Potter release parties. When was the last time you wanted to be at a bookstore at midnight? Jina hasn't been up until midnight since the Clinton administration! Also, can you remember this happening for any other book release *ever*? We can't.

Before Harry Potter, the prevailing thought was that young adult readers wouldn't want to read big books. In 2006, books targeted to young adult readers averaged 174.5 pages. *Harry Potter and the Sorcerer's Stone* was over 300 pages, and that didn't stop teens from reading it. In fact, the longest book in the series was *Harry Potter and the Order of the Phoenix*, at over 800 pages. Since 2006, books targeted to this demographic now average 290 pages (Pierce, 2018). Harry Potter changed the world of reading.

Empowering Through Integration

Just as Harry Potter opened up a new world for many teens, we hope this book opens up a new perspective on how you serve your students in your English language arts class. We are teaching students who are wildly different from each other, and from the students we used to be. We are teaching them in a world where smartphones are at their fingertips and chatbots can do their homework. Models of compliance, passive learning, and teacher-directed instruction do not meet the needs of our kids. We have to change.

In addition to focusing on our standards in more innovative and equitable ways, we are required to implement numerous frameworks under the umbrella of inclusive practice. If you add up all these requirements and think of them as distinct frameworks, you will run out of time, patience, and, likely, your passion for teaching.

We agree that there's no time to pivot from rigorous academics to incorporate inclusive practice. That is why we advocate for integrating UDL, social-emotional learning, character education, and restorative practices into your literacy block by grounding each unit in high-quality texts, text sets, authentic speaking and writing opportunities, and lots of opportunities to build classroom communities that make students feel as though they belong.

Integrating these frameworks allows us to increase the academic outcomes for students while ensuring that they have authentic and meaningful experiences to build mastery in the four domains of literacy. The techniques in this book are tried and true and have significantly increased engagement and learning in our learning environments with at-promise youth.

Because our work begins and ends with the students we serve, we want to end this book by discussing the impact of comprehensive literacy instruction on two of our students.

Sophia's Story

Brianne Parker and Jina Poirier

Sophia walked into our classroom late and took her seat as she usually did three out of five school days a week. She would often stay after class until our professional day was over and help with organizing, filing, or just catching up on schoolwork. Sophia was bright, eager to learn, and attentive when in class, but inconsistent in her attendance. One day was different. She didn't have her hair curled and makeup done, and she was dressed in sweats and not in her cute fashionista attire.

She looked scared, confused, and anxious. When we were able to get a moment, we took Sophia into a private room and asked her if all was well. She immediately began to share that she had no place to live. Where she had been residing was no longer an option and she had no family willing or able to house her. As mandatory reporters, we had to report it and social services responded. We were honest about our obligation, shared empathy for her situation, and promised that we would continue to support her in our classroom.

We stood at the back door of the white Ford Taurus and opened it for Sophia. She turned, gave us a tearful smile, and said good-bye. As we stood in the parking lot and watched the car turn the corner, we knew that Sophia was now a ward of the state and, thank goodness, she was still our student.

It was as if the world had given us a flick to the ear to make sure we were listening. Yes, as teachers, we are tasked with instructing standards-based curricula and ensuring that students have a grasp on the subject matter. But for us, it's so much more than that, which is why we feel so strongly about teaching students about the importance of character. Sophia deserved to have adults in her life who demonstrated character traits such as honesty, empathy, and dependability; modeled those for her; and had shared language to talk about her situation. Sophia chose to be honest, responsible, and adaptable to her new situation, as scary and uncertain as it was. She was resilient and poised. We're not taking credit for her character here but sharing the importance of making room for discussions about character and modeling it in our learning environments. When students like Sophia face challenges in their lives, we have opportunities to create safe spaces that are rigorous, warm, and constant. We can do this not only by focusing on social-emotional learning and helping students reflect on and honor their character, but also by using restorative practices that allow students like Sophia to speak their truth and ask for support when they need it.

Audrey's Story

Audrey was a young girl who faced some significant barriers. Her mom was a known drug user, and her dad wasn't in the picture. Audrey bounced around the social services system, moving from group homes to foster care to reunification and back again. She was a survivor, no doubt, but she had learned to survive no matter the cost.

At school, Audrey would poke fun at others' weaknesses, become confrontational in an uncomfortable situation, and often shut down when faced with nonpreferred tasks and requests. Audrey had compassion, perseverance, and empathy, but the traits weren't being expressed to her favor. She persevered in fighting for her and her siblings to be placed together in their constant moves, but when encouraged to persevere through difficult school and social situations, she became combative. She was compassionate to her younger siblings' feelings and empathetic to her mother's addiction struggles. As much as it was our job to support Audrey with literacy, we also had an incredible opportunity to help her celebrate her strengths and use them to propel herself and her siblings toward success, however they defined it. Enter the magic of restorative circles!

Audrey had taken part in three novel studies before her teacher started *Forgotten Fire* by Adam Bagdasarian. It tells the story of a young Armenian boy named Vahan Kenderian and his family, who lived in the city of Bitlis in Eastern Turkey during the early 1900s. The book provides a vivid portrayal of the horrors of the Armenian genocide, including the forced marches, concentration camps, and massacres that claimed the lives of an estimated 1.5 million Armenians. It also explores themes of identity, survival, and the power of hope in the face of unimaginable adversity. Based on past experiences, Audrey's teacher was prepared for another bout of oppositional defiance, disruption, and zero buy-in. According to the teacher, this book was a million miles away from Audrey's chaotic lifestyle and experiences. Thankfully, the exact opposite was true.

Almost from the start of the novel, Audrey was not only actively engaged in the restorative circle discussions, but actually added amazing insight and perceptions that others in class had not considered. At first, the teacher and her fellow classmates were virtually silent. They had never seen this side of Audrey and there were naturally some trust issues. However, this was quickly eradicated in favor of rich discussions and thoughtful insight. Without realizing it, Audrey's teacher had created an environment through circles that promoted fairness, respect, and trust. It just took time for Audrey to feel comfortable enough to embrace it.

While her teacher thought that *Forgotten Fire* was going to be far too foreign for Audrey, the themes and experiences in the book spoke to her. The main character in the book lost both of his parents and fought to keep his other siblings alive. Sadly, he was the only survivor. Was this not Audrey's biggest fear? She fought tirelessly to protect her siblings. Though not facing genocide, Audrey certainly could identify with the adversity faced by the characters in the novel. And while her connection was associated with negative experiences, it was still a connection. Audrey began to change from the reading of that novel. Initially, she just took part in the restorative circles, but within a week her academic work associated with the novel began to improve. She made a connection to the novel, and this, when conducted effectively, is the magic of restorative circles.

As we have learned previously, when students feel safe, respected, and valued, they're more likely to engage in literacy activities and take risks with their writing and reading. Restorative practices can help to build these positive relationships by focusing on repairing harm, building empathy, and promoting dialogue. This is exactly what happened to Audrey. She finally felt safe enough that she was able to add a great deal to the circles when she found a book that spoke to her. Congratulations are in order to the teacher as well. Despite months of negative behaviors, disruptions, and outbursts, the teacher forged ahead and kept the circles operating effectively. Some of these successes may not happen overnight, but if it can work for Audrey it can work for all. As Nelson Mandela said, "It always seems impossible until it's done."

References

Anderson, J. (2019, August 28). Hooked on classics. *Harvard Ed.* gse
.harvard.edu/news/ed/19/08/hooked-classics

Anzaldúa, G. (1987). *Borderlands = La frontera: The new mestiza.* San
Francisco: Spinsters/Aunt Lute.

Barnum, M. (2019). Major new study finds restorative justice led to
safer schools, but hurt black students' test scores. *Chalkbeat.* https://
www.chalkbeat.org/2019/1/4/21106465/major-new-study-finds
-restorative-justice-led-to-safer-schools-but-hurt-black-students
-test-scores

Beck, I. L., McKeown, M. G., & Kucan, L. (2013). *Bringing words to life:
Robust vocabulary instruction.* 2nd edition. Guilford Press.

Bouronikos, V. (2021). How to approach digital natives in education.
Institute of Entrepreneurship Development (iED). https://ied.eu
/project-updates/how-to-approach-digital-natives-in-education/

Bowen, B. (1993). Using conferences to support the writing process.
In A. M. Penrose & B. M. Sitko, *Hearing ourselves think: Cognitive
research in the college writing classroom (social and cognitive studies
in writing and literacy).* Oxford Press.

Boyles-Watson, C., & Pranis, K. (2020). *Circle forward: Building a restorative school community.* Living Justice Press.

Bradley, R. H. & Corwyn, R. F. (2002). Socioeconomic status and child
development. *Annual Review of Psychology, 53,* 371–99. 10.1146
/annurev.psych.53.100901.135233

Buffum, A., Mattos, M., & Weber, C. (2010). The why behind RTI. *Educational Leadership, 68*(2), 10–16.

Campbell, K. H. (2014). Beyond the five-paragraph essay. *Educational Leadership, 71*(7), 60–65. https://www.ascd.org/el/articles/beyond -the-five-paragraph-essay

CASEL. (2019). 3 signature practices playbook: A tool that supports systematic SEL. https://schoolguide.casel.org/resource/three -signature-sel-practices-for-the-classroom/

Character Counts. (n.d.). Why is character education important? https:// charactercounts.org/

Chardin, M., & Novak, K. (2020). *Equity by design: Delivering on the power and promise of UDL.* Corwin Press.

Chardin, M., & Vasquez, E. (2022). What are restorative practices? Novak Education. https://www.novakeducation.com/blog/what-are -restorative-practices

Costello, B., Wachtel, J., & Wachtel, T. (2010). *The restorative circles in schools: Building community and enhancing learning.* International Institute of Restorative Practices.

Cunningham, A. E., & Stanovich, K. E. (2001). What reading does for the mind. *Journal of Direct Instruction, 1*(2), 137–49.

Darling-Hammond, L., Hyler, M. E., & Gardner, M. (2017). *Effective teacher professional development.* Palo Alto, CA: Learning Policy Institute.

DuFour, R., & Reeves, D. (2016, March 1). The futility of PLC lite. *Phi Delta Kappan, 97*(6), 69–71. https://kappanonline.org/the-futility-of -plc-lite/

Durlak, J. A., Weissberg, R. P., Dymnicki, A. B., Taylor, R. D., & Schell-inger, K. (2011). The impact of enhancing students' social and emotional learning: A meta-analysis of school-based universal inter-ventions. *Child Development, 82,* 405–32. https://doi.org/10.1111 /j.1467-8624.2010.01564.x

Eksi, G. Y. (2012). Peer review versus teacher feedback in process writ-ing: How effective? *International Journal of Applied Educational Studies, 13*(1), 33–48.

Emdin, C. (2021). *Ratchetdemic: Reimagining academic success.* Beacon Press.

Fredricks, J. A., Blumenfeld, P. C., & Paris, A. H. (2004). School engage-ment: Potential of the concept, state of the evidence. *Review of*

Educational Research, 74(1), 59–109. https://doi.org/10.3102
/003465430740010 59

Graham, S. (2019). Changing how writing is taught. *Review of Research in Education, 43*(1), 277–303. https://doi.org/10.3102/0091732X18821125

Hart, B., & Risley, T. R. (1995). *Meaningful differences in the everyday experience of young American children.* Paul H. Brookes Publishing Company.

Hattie, J. (2018). Hattie ranking: 252 influences and effect sizes related to student achievement. Visible Learning. https://visible-learning. org/hattie-ranking-influences-effect-sizes-learning-achievement/

Hinkle, R., Parker, B., Reed, J., & Wolff, A. (2019). Where imagination meets reality: Empowering students to be lifelong readers. *Journal of Juvenile Court, Community and Alternative School Administrators of California, 32*, 30–35.

hooks, b. (2014). *Teaching to transgress.* Routledge.

Hoy, A. W. (2000). Changes in teacher efficacy during the early years of teaching. Paper presented at the Annual Meeting of the American Educational Research Association, New Orleans.

Institute of Educational Sciences. (2019). Teaching elementary school students to be effective writers. https://ies.ed.gov/ncee/wwc/Docs /PracticeGuide/WWC_Elem_Writing_PG_Dec182018.pdf

Iyengar, S. S., & Lepper, M. R. (2000). When choice is demotivating: Can one desire too much of a good thing? *Journal of Personality and Social Psychology, 79*(6), 995–1006. https://psycnet.apa.org/doi /10.1037/0022-3514.79.6.995

Knudson, K. C. (2022). What do we really mean by social emotional learning? Novak Education. https://www.novakeducation.com/blog /what-do-we-really-mean-by-social-emotional-learning-clarifying-sel

Kolb, L. (2017). *Learning first, technology second: The educator's guide to designing authentic lessons.* International Society for Technology in Education.

Kolb, L. (2020). Triple E framework models. https://www.tripleeframe work.com/framework-models.html

Literacy Design Collaborative. (2018). Student work rubric: Infor- mational/explanatory task, grades 9–12. https://s.ldc.org/u /e7fr7huinkm84pgiinmu2xmu4

Louis, A. (2013). *Predicting text quality: Metrics for content, organization and reader interest.* Publicly Accessible Penn Dissertations 665. [Doctoral dissertation, Penn University]. https://repository.upenn .edu/edissertations/665

Marzano, R. (2004). Building background knowledge for academic achievement: Research on what works in schools (professional development). Association for Supervision & Curriculum Development (ASCD).

McChesney, C., Covey, S., & Huling, J. (2012). *The 4 disciplines of execution: Achieving your wildly important goals.* Simon and Schuster.

McTighe, J., & Wiggins, G. (2013). *Essential questions: Opening doors to student understanding.* ASCD.

Meyer, A., Rose, D. H., & Gordon, D. (2014). *Universal design for learning: Theory and practice.* CAST Professional Publishing.

Miller, M. (2015). *Ditch that textbook: Free your teaching and revolutionize your classroom.* Dave Burgess Consulting.

Minor, C. (2018). *We got this: Equity, access, and the quest to be who our students need us to be.* Heinemann Educational Books.

National Academies of Sciences, Engineering, and Medicine. (2018). *How people learn II.* National Academies Press.

Novak, K., & Rodriguez, K. (2016). *Universally designed leadership: Applying UDL to systems and schools.* CAST Professional Publishing.

Novak, K., & Woodlock, M. (2022). *UDL playbook for school and district leaders.* CAST Professional Publishing.

Novak, K., (2022). *UDL now.* 3rd edition. CAST Professional Publishing.

Patall, E. A., Cooper, H., & Robinson, J. C. (2008). The effects of choice on intrinsic motivation and related outcomes: A meta-analysis of research findings. *Psychological Bulletin, 134*(2), 270–300.

Patall, E., Cooper, H., & Wynn, S. (2010). The effectiveness and relative importance of choice in the classroom. *Journal of Educational Psychology, 102,* 896–915.

Pickering, D. J., & Marzano, R. J. (2005). *Building academic vocabulary: Teacher's manual.* Alexandria, VA: ASCD.

Pierce, S. (2018, August 30). Five ways Harry Potter changed children's literature. *Chattanooga Times Free Press.* https://www.timesfree press.com/news/2018/aug/30/five-ways-harry-potter-changed -childrens-lite/

Pierson, R. (2013). Every kid needs a champion. [Video]. TED Talk. http://www.ted.com/talks/rita_pierson_every_kid_needs _a_champion

Prince, E. A. (2021). *I sued the school system.* [Video]. YouTube. https:// www.youtube.com/watch?v=dqTTojTija8&feature=emb_imp_woyt

Protheroe, N. (2008). Teacher efficacy and why does it matter? Retrieved from http://www.naesp.org/sites/default/files/resources/1/Pdfs /Teacher_Efficacy_What_is_it_and_Does_it_Matter.pdf

Ossola, A. (2014). Why kids won't quit technology. *The Atlantic.* https:// www.theatlantic.com/education/archive/2014/12/why-kids-wont -quit-tech/383575/

Revell, M. (2020). Restorative instructional practices: (Un)interrupting the teaching of restorative approaches. In S. Polat and G. Günça-vdı, *Empowering multiculturalism and peacebuilding in schools* (pp. 86–111). IGI Global.

Schwartz, B. (2005, July). The paradox of choice [Video]. TED Conferences. https://www.ted.com/talks/barry_schwartz_the_paradox _of_choice/

Schwanenflugel, P. J., & Flanagan, N. (2017, February 28). Three myths about "reading levels" and why you shouldn't fall for them. *Psychology Today.* https://www.psychologytoday.com/us/blog/reading -minds/201702/three-myths-about-reading-levels

Sinek, S. (2009). *Start with why: How great leaders inspire everyone to take action.* Penguin.

Small, G. (2009, July 22). Techno addicts. *Psychology Today.* https:// www.psychologytoday.com/us/blog/brain-bootcamp/200907 /techno-addicts

Sparks, S. D. (2019, November 8). Screen time up as reading scores drop. Is there a link? *Education Week.* https://www.edweek.org /teaching-learning/screen-time-up-as-reading-scores-drop-is -there-a-link/2019/11

Springer, S. E., Harris, S., & Dole, J. A. (2017). From surviving to thriving: Four research-based principles to build students' reading interest. *The Reading Teacher, 71*(1), 43–50. https://doi.org/10.1002/trtr.1581

Tompkins, G. E. (2018). *Literacy for the 21st century: A balanced approach,* 7th edition. Pearson.

Tucker, C., & Novak, K. (2022). *The shift to student-led.* San Diego: Impress.

Twenge, J. M., Martin, G. N., & Spitzberg, B. H. (2019). Trends in U.S. adolescents' media use, 1976–2016: The rise of digital media, the decline of TV, and the (near) demise of print. *Psychology of Popular Media Culture, 8*(4), 329–45.

Wacks, Y., & Weinstein, A. M. (2021). Excessive smartphone use is associated with health problems in adolescents and young adults. *Frontiers in Psychiatry,* 12, https://doi.org/10.3389/fpsyt.2021.669042

Watchel, T., & McCold, P. (2000). Restorative justice in everyday life. In J. Braithwaite and H. Strang (Eds.), *Restorative justice in civil society* (pp. 117–25). New York: Cambridge University Press.

Wilson, L.O. (2001). Bloom's taxonomy revised. Understanding the revised version of Bloom's taxonomy. https://thesecondprinciple.com/essential-teaching-skills/blooms-taxonomy-revised/

Worthy, J. (1996). A matter of interest: Literature that hooks reluctant readers and keeps them reading. *The Reading Teacher, 50*(3), 204–12.

Index

Acknowledgments

Katie

To all my besties at CAST, I wouldn't be where I am today without you. To David Rose and David Gordon (my Pawtucket brother), thank you for taking a chance on me when I was a seventh-grade teacher trying to find a way to better serve my students. *UDL Now* was my first book, and today, this makes lucky #13. It has been a hell of a ride, sharing the power and promise of UDL. To Billie, you are such a brilliant editor and remind me of the power of the writing process. Every time I think I may be close to being done, you are in my ear whispering, "Not yet." Your work on the reorganization of this book has been brilliant.

To my amazing coauthors, thank you from the bottom of my heart for sharing your work with me and the world. From the time we met in that little conference room, I knew that we needed to elevate and celebrate your work. You all unequivocally believe that every student is capable of learning at high levels when we leverage inclusive practices. UDL is not the goal, but rather a vehicle that helps you serve students so that they can reach their full potential as learners and leaders. Your stories about your students and their growth and success is inspiring. They are so lucky to have you, and goodness, you are lucky to have each other. Maybe someday, if you're lucky, Ryan will take you out for a sail on the Caspian.

I couldn't do any of this work without my fam. Lindie, you are my bestest friend, my sister-love, my designer, my conscience, and the person who keeps me real when I have megalomaniac ideas. Love you!! To Lon/Don, my husband and his fake assistant, thank you for doing so much for the house, yard, dog, and kids so I can write. It is such a passion and I love that you create so much space for me to do it. Maybe someday I will repay you by doing a load of laundry. And to my heart: Torin, Aylin, Brecan, and Boden, my hope for you is that you fall in love with literacy and the power of words. As Clint Smith said in his TED Talk, "The Danger of Silence," my hope for you is that you always read critically, write consciously, speak clearly, and tell your truth.

Ryan

Let me begin by thanking my mom, who has been in my corner my entire life. You have always been my biggest supporter and have shown unconditional love even when I probably did not deserve it. As I have gotten older, I have come to understand and appreciate the sacrifices and lengths you have taken on my behalf and for that I am eternally grateful. I'd also like to give a shout-out to my dad and stepmom, who instilled in me the importance of an education and value of perseverance. I am sure they thought that I was oblivious to their influence during my teenage years, but it slipped into a mind gap somewhere. Acknowledgment would not be complete without a huge high-five to my cousins, Rick and Jeniel. I know that the family tree says cousins, but you are both siblings in my world and I love that you are both in my life. On a more somber note, thanks cannot be administered without mentioning my Grandpa Mick and my Uncle Bob. Neither is with us any longer, but I carry you with me daily. Grandpa, you taught me all of the valuable lessons one needs to succeed in life. Uncle Bob, we shared a love of literature and travel, a sense of humor, and of course Manhattans. This book would never have been possible without our time together.

Besides my comrades in the Caspian Sea, I would like to thank all of my friends. While there are too many to mention individually, I'd be remiss without referencing a few. To Austin, David, and Jerry, I think we only hang out together because no one else can stand us. Not a big surprise, though; our wives can barely tolerate us. To Jason, let's just say it's been quite a ride. I've enjoyed growing up together almost as much as I have relished the trouble we have gotten in throughout the years. I wish I could mention a few, but it would be more beneficial to myself and my fellow authors if this book remained G-rated. Looking forward to many more years of unadulterated debauchery. Finally, a quick nod to Les Amis restaurant. Thanks for allowing me to sit and write this book in an environment where I always feel welcome and at home.

To the ACE team: Wow! What a long, strange trip it has been. I cannot tell you how fortunate I am to have met you all. I have never worked with any other colleagues that would have made this dream possible. We not only work well together but also complement one another's strengths and weaknesses. This reminds me of Jina's loquacious demeanor—still not sure if it's a strength or a weakness, but we make it work! Also, a quick tip of the hat to Katy and Jane. Your support and enthusiasm for this project was not only palpable but helped to keep us on track and grounded. And Katy, we forgive you for trying to proofread our half-finished manuscript. Of course, none of this would have been possible without the amazing Dr. Katie Novak. Had you not come into our room during one of our early ACE presentations, we'd all still be looking at a blank computer screen with bemused, befuddled, and helpless expressions. You were the Turkish Delight in this whole process and your leadership and genius made this happen. You rock. Get ready to visit the Caspian Sea!!!

Finally, I want to give the biggest thanks to my wife and kids. Maria, you make me a better person every day and I am so grateful to have you as my partner in life. Sorry for having to put up with me and feeling like you have three kids instead of two. Thank you for always being there for me, for making our home a place of comfort, and for being the best wife I could ever hope for. I love you more than words could ever express. To Lukas and Nohl, I cannot tell you how proud I am to have two of the best sons a dad could ever hope for. I love you for all the ways we are the same and especially for the ways that we are different.

Brianne

To my grandmother, my granny, my guardian angel, my biggest fan, and a lover of all romance and mystery novels: thank you for all those late nights of reading together and the many, many trips to the bookstore! Thank you to my sister, Autumn, for all my early morning phone calls and words of encouragement. To my Noah, the world is a better place because you are in it; never change. To my Ethan, keep up those drawings, you *will* be a published illustrator one day!

To my parents, who encouraged my love for literacy from a young age. It all began on the little training potty with a Twinkie in one hand and a book in the other. Thank you for showing me that reading is truly the key to unlocking the world.

To my amazingly talented ACE team, you guys ROCK! I would not have wanted to go on this journey with anyone else, except maybe "Henry" (ha!). Truly, you guys are phenomenal and I have such admiration for your dedication to our craft. Dr. Katie Novak, there are not enough words to describe the gratitude and appreciation I have for taking a chance on us. From the moment we first met, I was in awe of your work, poise, expertise, and pure love for literacy. Writing this book with you has definitely accomplished a bucket list item!

Most importantly, I could not have done any of this without the love and support of my family. My husband, Andy, who has always supported and encouraged me to follow my dreams, you are my biggest supporter and I am grateful to do this life with you! Thank you and I love you with all my heart. To my greatest accomplishments, Clare (15), Dean (13), and Audrey (6), I pray that you find a love for literacy and you continue to be you! Remember, get comfortable being uncomfortable and you can take on the world. I love you!!!!

Jina

To my superwoman single mom: You taught me that education is invaluable and that it's the one thing that no one can take away from me. You have been my first and forever teacher in life, and I wouldn't be who I am today without you as my mom. Your unwavering belief in me and being my loudest cheerleader in life continues to inspire me. I am eternally grateful to be your daughter.

To my family: Murchison, Crimi, Williams, Posey, and Goehle— wow, we have a big family! I intentionally stuck to using last names to ensure that I didn't miss anyone, as we all know how easily that could happen. I want to express my gratitude to all of you for teaching me the value of inclusion and acceptance, and to always look for the good in others. Some time ago, I bought a T-shirt in support of our local foster youth; it had the phrase "no labels, just family" This phrase perfectly describes our unique and special bond, and having both my adopted and birth family in my life is an honor and privilege. I truly believe that this unique and special blessing allows me to connect and grow with the students I work with each day. Words can never express the love I have for all of you!

To my girls who I wouldn't want to "life" without. Kat, you have been my "ride or die" for over four decades. Your unwavering love of books and ability to lose yourself in their pages has always been a source of inspiration for me. Ronnie, I have always been struck by your nonjudgmental nature and your unconditional love and acceptance of who I am. Your friendship has been an incredible gift in my life. Nadia, as my teaching partner for many years, you have challenged me to grow and evolve as an educator. Looking back, I realize that we had so much to learn, but your encouragement and support have been invaluable. Thank you all for your love, friendship, and unwavering support.

To all of my coauthors, this has been an incredible ride, and it's only the beginning! Thank you for pushing me outside of my comfort zone and providing me with a safe place to have big ideas. Dr. Novak (or, as we know you, the other Katie), there are no words that can express my gratitude. I still pinch myself, thinking that the author and educator I low-key stalked on Twitter saw something in our work and decided to take a chance on us! Huge thanks to our Boss Lady Directors, Katy and Lynn! Sometimes, all a team needs is a yes from the boss to create outside the lines. You both not only said yes, but also encouraged and supported all of our crazy ideas on integration! I am grateful for the "Doney in my pocket" that reminds me to focus on what's in my #ROI. I will continue to "water the flowers and not the rocks" on my journey in education. Thank you for believing in me and helping me to grow.

To my "Pear Tree" aka my husband, Michael: thanks for being the man of my dreams! When I doubt myself, you are the one reminding me to believe in my ability and to push through. On the days I am overwhelmed, your reply is always the same: "How do you eat an elephant? One bite at a time." As many times as you say it, you're always right! See what I did there? I just literally put in print that you're always right! You're welcome. :) I love you with all my heart.

Anne

To my amazing, beautiful, and strong-willed mom. I couldn't have gotten to where I am today without you. You taught me that when one door closes, another opens . . . or maybe a window, or you look for the secret passageway. You taught me to think outside the box, which has become something I teach my students and fellow educators. To my Grandma, whom I know is my guardian angel and is always looking out for me: thank you for continuing to guide me. To my dad and sister, thank you for always being there for me when I needed you most.

To my fellow ACE team coauthors, I don't know how I got so lucky to be a part of such an amazing team. I consider you all family. To Dr. Katie Novak, thank you so much for bringing me on this wild journey. Writing this book was a master class in the literary industry. I am in awe of your talents and expertise.

If you had told the little girl growing up in Glendale, California, that one day she would be a coauthor of a book, she probably would not have believed you. This goes to show that anything is possible if you truly believe in yourself, are surrounded by a great support system, and are always looking for that secret tunnel around the roadblock in front of you. I fully believe that everything happens for a reason. The challenges I faced throughout my life have brought me here. And I wouldn't change a thing.

About the Authors

Katie Novak, EdD, is an internationally renowned education consultant, author, graduate instructor at the University of Pennsylvania, and a former assistant superintendent of schools in Massachusetts. She has over 20 years of experience in teaching and administration, earned a doctorate in curriculum and teaching, and has published 13 books. Katie designs and presents workshops both nationally and internationally focusing on the implementation of inclusive practices, Universal Design for Learning (UDL), multitiered systems of support, and universally designed leadership. Her work has impacted educators worldwide as her contributions and collaborations have built upon the foundation for an educational framework that is critical for student success. Katie is the author of the best-selling books, *UDL Now! A Teacher's Guide to Applying Universal Design for Learning in Today's Classrooms, Innovate Inside the Box* (with George Couros), *Equity by Design* (with Mirko Chardin), and *UDL and Blended Learning* (with Catlin Tucker). Her work has been highlighted in many publications, including *Forbes, Edutopia, Cult of Pedagogy, Language Magazine, NAESP Principal, ADDitude Magazine, Commonwealth Magazine, The Inclusion Lab, Think Inclusive,* the *Huffington Post, Principal Leadership, District Administrator, ASCD Education Update,* and *School Administrator*.

After years as a merchant seaman in the Caspian Sea, **Ryan Hinkle, MA,** became a teacher with the Orange County Department of Education, Alternative, Community, & Correctional Educational Schools and Services (ACCESS) program. In 2016, Ryan accepted a position as the ELA TOSA for the ACCESS program, where he supported staff with the implementation of ELA standards and the promotion of differentiated instruction and UDL. Ryan was one of the initial creators of ACCESS 2 Character Education (ACE) and continues to develop and promote its curriculum. During his TOSA reign, Ryan had the unique opportunity to teach a group of Afghan refugees who were part of the Afghanistan diaspora following the reintroduction of the Taliban in 2021. Although these Afghan students were displaced and living out of hotels throughout Orange County, California, their willingness and enthusiasm to learn and excel had a profound impact on Ryan and helped to further mold his educational mission statement. In 2022, his TOSA position was discontinued and Ryan went back to the classroom, where he continues working with at-promise youth. Ryan has been involved with alternative education since 1999. He holds a BA in psychology, a BS in bio writing, and an MA in education. While he relishes his time as an educator, he looks forward to returning to the frigid waters of the Caspian Sea at some point.

Brianne Parker, MEd, began her career in education as an instructional aide with the Orange County Department of Education, Alternative, Community, & Correctional Educational Schools and Services (ACCESS) program, while finishing her BA. Initially, Brianne wasn't sure that the world of education was her destined career path. After just a few short months working with at-promise youth, she knew that this was where her passion and heart lie. Brianne became a teacher just six months after beginning as an instructional aide and has since held the positions of classroom teacher, EL TOSA, program specialist, and assistant principal.

She has also taught adult ESL classes and college courses. Brianne was one of the initial creators of ACCESS 2 Character Education (ACE) and continues to develop and promote its curriculum. She has presented the ACE curriculum along with her colleagues at several local, state, and national conferences. In 2022, Brianne had the privilege of teaching displaced Afghan refugee students along with her colleagues in makeshift classrooms in hotel rooms throughout Orange County. This experience solidified Brianne's passion for teaching, especially with at-promise youth. Currently, she is back in the classroom and teaching with the ACCESS program's Pacific Coast High School. She has 22 years of experience in alternative education and holds a BA in English literature and a MEd in education. She is a Level 1 Google Certified Educator.

Jina Poirier, MEd, is an innovative educator with a passion for incorporating technology and creativity in a leadership capacity. With 19 years of experience inspiring and engaging at-promise youth, Jina has fostered an environment where learning and professional growth has affected both students and staff. She believes in the power of integration of proven practices! Jina has a proven track record of designing and implementing engaging, student-centered lessons that challenge and inspire learners of all levels. Jina was one of the initial creators of ACCESS 2 Character Education (ACE) and continues to develop and promote its curriculum. She taps into her expertise in the areas of academic interventions, assessment, restorative practices, and UDL in her current role as Coordinator, Accountability, Assessment, and Academic Interventions with the Orange County Department of Education, Alternative, Community, & Correctional Educational Schools and Services (ACCESS) program.

Prior to her current position, Jina held the positions of classroom teacher and program specialist for EL Services writing and training teachers on integrated and designated language supports for emergent bilingual students. She has a BS in human services and a MEd in education. Throughout her time in education, she has had the privilege of working in many unique learning environments. Jina believes that if we can design engaging curriculum and delivery for the most restrictive learning environments (such as juvenile hall), we can make it come alive in all settings! Jina is a Trainer of Trainers in Restorative Practices trained through the International Institute for Restorative Practices (IIRP).

Anne Wolff, MEd, began her career in education working as an instructional aide in technology at Huntington Beach High School and Huntington Beach Adult School from 2010 to 2015. In January 2015, Anne was hired by the Orange County Department of Education in the alternative education program Alternative, Community, & Correctional Educational Schools and Services (ACCESS) as Educational Technology User Support Assistant. Over the course of a 13-year career, she has built her professional reputation utilizing expertise in education, arts, media, entertainment, and information/communication technologies on three principles: hard work, efficiency, and continuous improvement. She supports students and staff with technology in the classroom as well as instructing students and staff on the use of the current digital tools. Anne was one of the initial creators of ACCESS 2 Character Education (ACE) and continues to develop and promote its curriculum. She has presented at conferences and coauthored articles with her fellow ACE team members. She holds a BA in political science, a BS in multimedia design technology, and an MS in educational and instructional technology. She has also earned CTE credentials in information and communication technologies, and arts, media, and entertainment. She is a Level 1 and 2 Google Certified Educator. In 2022, over a four-month period, Anne had the privilege of working with displaced families from Afghanistan. She, along with an amazing group of educators, created makeshift classrooms in five hotel rooms across Orange County, California.

She was in charge of teaching the students and parents how to use the school laptops and different educational programs. Most had never seen a computer before. By the end of the program, the Afghan families had a basic understanding of how to use the digital tools and take their newfound skills on to their next journey. Anne will be forever grateful that she was able to be part of such an amazing experience.

One of Anne's strengths is that she is able to look at things from different angles. She jokes that her tombstone will say "Think Outside the Box." She loves the challenge of incorporating new and innovative ways to use educational technology. If a digital device or tool isn't working, leave it to her to figure out a creative solution.

More from ◯CAST Professional Publishing

ISBN 978-1-930583-82-5 (Print)
ISBN 978-1-930583-83-2 (ePub)
ISBN 978-1-943085-24-8 (Audiobook)
196 PAGES | © 2022

UDL Now! A Teacher's Guide to Applying Universal Design for Learning, Third Edition

By Katie Novak, with a foreword by George Couros

"Katie Novak's well-articulated know-how, about how to put UDL into practice, has helped many thousands of educators . . . She can describe what she does without evaporating the awe, the joy, or the sublimity of what great teaching is really like."

—DAVID H. ROSE, co-founder of CAST

ISBN 978-1-943085-16-3 (Print)
ISBN 978-1-943085-17-0 (ePub)
208 PAGES | © 2024

¡DUA Ahora!: Una guía del profesor para aplicar ed Diseño Universal para el Aprendizaje, Tercera Edición

By Katie Novak, con un prólogo de George Couros

Katie Novak, una voz internacional líder en el Diseño Universal para el Aprendizaje (DUA), brinda conocimientos prácticos y estrategias inteligentes para ayudar a los educadores a tener éxito en la enseñanza de todos los estudiantes en el mundo pospandémico.

ISBN 978-1-930583-95-5 (Print)
ISBN 978-1-930583-94-8 (ePub)
224 PAGES | © 2022

Transform Your Teaching with Universal Design for Learning: Six Steps to Jumpstart Your Practice

Jennifer L. Pusateri

"Putting UDL into practice can be daunting for teachers who are just starting out. Jennifer L. Pusateri puts them at ease as she suggests step-by-step strategies to transform our teaching with this powerful framework."

—ANDRATESHA FRITZGERALD, founder of Building Blocks of Brilliance LLC

For more information, visit **www.castpublishing.org** or wherever books are sold. For bulk orders, email **publishing@cast.org**.

More from ⃝CAST Professional Publishing

ISBN 978-1-930583-98-6 (Print)
ISBN 978-1-930583-99-3 (ePub)
242 PAGES | © 2023

Elevating Co-teaching with Universal Design for Learning, Revised and Expanded Edition

By Elizabeth Stein, with a foreword by Marilyn Friend

"This book is an enlightening roadmap for teaching partners who are working diligently to keep their expectations high while taking into account all the different abilities their students bring to the classroom."

—MARILYN FRIEND, Professor Emerita, University of North Carolina at Greensboro

ISBN 978-1-930583-70-2 (Print)
ISBN 978-1-930583-71-9 (ePub)
192 PAGES | © 2022

Antiracism and Universal Design for Learning: Building Expressways to Success

By Andratesha Fritzgerald, with a foreword by Samaria Rice

"Fritzgerald offers very practical suggestions for making inclusion, antiracism, and the acceptance of differences the first and most important step in lesson planning. . . . This book gives me hope that, in education, we can begin to eliminate the violence of academic and social prejudice that kills the spirit of our babies and belittles the needs and experiences of people of color."

—SAMARIA RICE, founder and CEO of the Tamir Rice Foundation

ISBN 978-1-943085-00-2 (Print)
ISBN 978-1-943085-01-9 (ePub)
144 PAGES | © 2023

Building Executive Function and Motivation in the Middle Grades: A Universal Design for Learning Approach

By Susanne Croasdaile

"This book reads easily in a sitting, but like the best instructional practices, can be broken into chunks so that teachers can quickly implement meaningful, research-based routines to support executive function in their classrooms. I've personally witnessed teachers using these strategies, and the difference they've made in their classrooms is remarkable

—JEFF BOARMAN, Assistant Principal, Carter G. Woodson Middle School

For more information, visit **www.castpublishing.org** or wherever books are sold. For bulk orders, email **publishing@cast.org**.

MORE FROM ⟲ CAST

CAST is a nonprofit education research and development organization that created the Universal Design for Learning framework and UDL Guidelines. Our mission is to transform education design and practice until learning has no limits.

CAST supports learners and educators at every level through a variety of offerings:

- Innovative professional development
- Accessibility and inclusive technology resources
- Research, design, and development of inclusive and effective solutions
- Credentials for Universal Design for Learning
- And much more

Visit *www.cast.org* to learn more.